STREET FIGHTING AT WALL AND BR
HG 4572 S28

D0787894

DATE DUE

JE 15			
FE 6			
MR 18			
DE 7 5 91			
OC 14 93			
JE 10			
8			
AP 27			

HG4572
S28

RIVERSIDE CITY COLLEGE
LIBRARY
Riverside, California

AP '81

DEMCO

STREET FIGHTING AT WALL AND BROAD

Marchand Sage

STREET FIGHTING

AT WALL AND BROAD

An Insider's Tale of Stock Manipulation

MACMILLAN PUBLISHING CO., INC.

New York

COLLIER MACMILLAN PUBLISHERS

London

Riverside Community College
Library
4800 Magnolia Avenue
Riverside, CA 92506

HG4572 .S28 1980
Sage, Marchand.
Street fighting at Wall and
Broad : an insider's tale o
stock manipulation

Copyright © 1980 by Marchand Sage

All rights reserved. No part of this book may be reproduced or

transmitted in any form or by any means, electronic or mechanical,

including photocopying, recording or by any information storage and

retrieval system, without permission in writing from the Publisher.

Macmillan Publishing Co., Inc.

866 Third Avenue, New York, N.Y.   10022

Collier Macmillan Canada, Ltd.

Library of Congress Cataloging in Publication Data
Sage, Marchand.
    Street fighting at Wall and Broad.
    1. Wall Street. I. Title.
— HG4572.S28   332.64′273   80–17587
    ISBN 0–02–606680–7

10 9 8 7 6 5 4 3 2 1

Designed by Jack Meserole

Printed in the United States of America

In remembrance of my father,

who taught us that the desire to understand

makes life a continuing romance

Contents

Preface

This work is a fable, which is variously defined as a fictitious narrative such as a story of supernatural happenings as in legend, or as a narrative enforcing some useful truth. Both descriptions are appropriate in some respects. All characters and events depicted in this book are fictitious (indeed, some activities described are actually illegal), and any resemblance to real persons, companies, or events is pure chance and coincidence. The happenings, however, are not supernatural—all stem from attitudes and habits of behavior that motivate traders, speculators, and investors on Wall Street. The purpose of the book is not to indict or condemn, but rather to entertain and inform.

Acknowledgments

Warmest thanks to my conscientious editor, Joyce Jack, whose numerous suggestions were invariably beneficial, and to Rayanna Simons, who contributed immeasurably to the organization and structure of the book.

PART I

1 The Arena

My occupation goes by assorted titles of varying complexity and pomposity. Some call it account executive, others registered representative, investment advisor, or investment counselor. Essentially, my success depends on the oldest commercial technique in the world: I try to buy wholesale and to sell at retail.

The distinction from most merchandisers is that I don't deal in tangibles. My inventory occupies no space on a display shelf, it is rarely if ever seen by the consumer, and it has no inherent usefulness. I am a professional buyer and seller of stocks on Wall Street. My objective is to buy at distress (read "low") prices before a change in vogue or the perceptions of the real world creates a more aggressive demand for my merchandise.

In order to buy stocks cheaply, I must be willing to bid for them when the competition is feeble. Wall Street is simply a public auction. When an item is in strong demand, the bidding is competitive and prices can move up with startling volatility. When a particular type of stock becomes in vogue (and much of my story concerns itself with how demand is created, controlled, and manipulated), those of us who bought early and cheaply, and then waited patiently, can sell at considerably higher "retail" prices.

It was once thought that you, "the public," was the sucker who bought our merchandise at peak prices. This is no longer necessarily true. The most frequent top-tick-payer is the so-called professional—the mutual fund or pension fund portfolio manager—who acts as an intermediary for the public. Paradoxically, the public, when acting for itself, has become amazingly sophisticated and shrewd, while those managers it has voluntarily (as in mutual funds or bank trust departments) or involuntarily (as in pension funds) chosen to act for it have a singularly undistinguished record of timing and selection. Probably the most realistic investor of all is the businessman who evaluates a public company the same way he does a private business. He looks at a share of a company and asks himself if he would buy the entire company at this specific market valuation.

My appearance hardly distinguishes me from hundreds of other men milling around the skyscraper-darkened canyons of lower Manhattan. Our suits are invariably dark, usually tailored with great care to look unfitted. Our hair is sometimes scarce in quantity and always cut with restraint and without overt styling. Our offices are to be found in those towering, marble-lobbied buildings that give the foot of the island its dramatically futuristic look. Once inside these massive structures, one has the feeling, by no accident, of solidity, prosperity, and sobriety. What actually goes on in our thickly carpeted sanctums is something else again.

I occupy a small, discreetly furnished suite of offices on Broad Street, on the fifty-first floor. The simple black lettering on the frosted double doors of my office suite reads CARLETON BROWN: INVESTMENT COUNSELING. Inside, the rosewood paneling is an unmistakable sign of quiet opulence, as is the spectacular view of the harbor. My private office is small. I require little equipment for what I do, and have arrived at a degree of success where I don't require props. On my desk are just three telephones and an electronic machine that provides a continuing instantaneous display of stock market activity during the day. The bookcases contain *Moody's* and *Standard & Poor's* references, *Value Line, Who's Who in Finance and Industry,* the *Wall Street Journal* index, and the *Registry of Directors and Executives.*

Gone are the hungry-eyed, lean days of my youth when, like the Ancient Mariner, I plucked at every passing sleeve (figuratively, of course), eager to acquire customers, whether they had $50 or $50,000 to invest. With no record of accomplishment, every decision then was a critical one, since clients were quick to switch allegiance from a counselor they believed was not performing.

Today my clientele is small in number but large in capital; they are select and powerful. I deal with just a few accounts and no longer seek or accept new clients. Reasonably affluent, my customers are professional business managers, successful lawyers or doctors, or heirs of wealth who are astute enough to realize their own limitations in the investment field. All must feel that I know my business well enough that I can be allowed complete freedom in making decisions and selecting investments. My customers do not share the popular belief that, while knowing nothing of the investment world, amateurs can casually enter the most merciless and sophisticated commercial arena in the world—Wall Street—and compete successfully with professionals who have devoted perhaps limited talents but probably unlimited energy, avarice, and effort to mastering their field.

I do very little trading in the conventional Wall Street sense. As a member of the Exchange, I do have trading privileges that allow me to go down to the floor of the Exchange and try to scalp fractions from active, volatile stocks while competing against a public that, unlike members of the Exchange, is burdened with heavy commission costs. When I was younger, I spent a period devoted to in-and-out trading.

It was remunerative, but, more importantly, it gave me insights that would prove invaluable in evoking a desired response among traders when I wanted them to accommodate my efforts to buy or to sell large quantities of stock.

In fact, I spend most of my time on the telephone or reading industry and corporation reports. My investment commitments rarely involve more than three situations at the same time. Quite often, the funds that I manage (and, incidentally, I pool my own capital with that of my clientele in all ventures) are reposing quietly in short-term treasury notes, securely awaiting the right vehicle and the right time. One of the most important basic principles for success in my field, learned from bitter and costly experience, is to avoid marginal situations, no matter how intense the temptation. For the trader, the most expensive form of amusement in the world is to buy or to sell a stock just to get "action" or to become "involved" when the resulting profit can, at best, be only marginal. This kind of behavior usually reflects the indecision or anxiety that afflicts speculators after a few decisions prove to be losers and they feel that they have lost their grip. When in doubt, don't play. This is straight from Uncle Carleton, and, believe me, he paid his tuition and he knows.

Why do traders usually die poor? Probably the reason is that they must have action and leap for the lure too often. Moreover, gambling one's ego on quick decisions must prove lethal in the end. When a trade is going right, the trader usually sells too soon. His probably unvoiced motive is that he has already proved the soundness of his judgment by initiating the trade. Now there is no further satisfaction to be derived from riding the situation. Thus, he runs to the next challenge in his constant desire to vindicate his judgment.

There are literally thousands of publicly owned corporations that have stocks listed on one or another of the major stock exchanges. On any given day there are dozens of these issues that are active and volatile, potentially profitable investment or trading vehicles on either the long or short side. The investment of some time and effort in exploration should provide sound opportunities for the rational and deliberate venturer. But—and this is one big qualification—there are times when even the most astute person, because of his temperament or uncertainty about general market or economic conditions, may find himself unsure of his own judgment concerning the course to follow with his capital. It is frequently at this time that the stock-player becomes that most odious of Wall Street animals, the poll-taker. Knowing little and thinking nothing, he polls others of perhaps even less knowledge and intelligence. He finally comes out with either a consensus or a single opinion that strikes his fancy, acts accordingly, and makes the wrong decision.

One must remember that the stock market is as unsentimental as the weather report. If not functioning with maximum clarity and conviction, one shouldn't play the game. Stop, reassess the situation, retire momentarily to a good book or to the late show. "Invite your soul" as Thoreau advised, but leave your capital intact. It may not be doing anything spectacular, perhaps just collecting some modest percent in Treasuries, but it also is not eloping with some collapsing stock issue.

Another of the simplest but wisest of Wall Street maxims is that it is easier to make one decision than two. If your capital is in Mea Culpa, Inc., and you want to buy Magma Capital, you first have to decide to sell your "loser" before you can decide to buy a potential winner. And that first decision is often too painful to make.

But let's get down to my business, which is using the techniques by which stocks are made to go up and down, and maybe up and down again, depending upon what the professionals want them to do. I propose to give you the history of a specific investment situation that provided me with an array of adventures, anxieties, and pleasures. I don't know whether there are any real heroes or villains in this drama, and I fear I myself don't show to advantage in the telling. My consolation will be ample if the reader finds the experience useful in his or her own investment activities.

2 The Quarry

For some time I had been casually following the market action of the American Building Products Company. My primary efforts—and capital—had been committed elsewhere, but I had kept abreast of ABP ever since it had been brought to my attention half a dozen years earlier by an associate, Fred Confrer, who had long shared my predilection for asset-rich, prosaic companies. The name of the company was as unremarkable as its basic business, that of making plywood, finished lumber, and related products used in the construction of new homes and by the do-it-yourself home maintenance and improvement industry.

The business-school graduate would classify ABP as a "vertically integrated enterprise." It wasn't engaged in only a single stage of transforming timber into building materials; its activities extended vertically through each successive phase from growing trees, to cutting and finishing lumber, and ultimately to distribution through a nationwide network of wholesalers and jobbers.

American Building Products had been in business for over five decades. The venerable organization had been founded by the grandfather of the present chief executive officer in the dynamic period of economic growth that preceded the First World War. Grandpa Founder's empire began with the acquisition of thousands of acres of virgin timberland in the Wisconsin-Michigan area through means that are best not examined too fastidiously.

During the first two decades of its existence, ABP expanded rapidly. From a tough and shrewd former lumberjack, Grandpa evolved into an industrial tycoon of the classic school: more prosaic than flamboyant, and still devoted to the Calvinist principles of hard work and limited play. After those first golden years, the growth of the company slowed down, partly because of the natural loss of momentum any enterprise sustains as it reaches a degree of maturity. But more significantly, the drive and energy that characterized Grandpa Founder in his business career were less pronounced in his successors. The next generation opted more for spending, senator-making, and martini-sipping—an evolutionary leap from the high-stakes gamesmanship and arduous efforts that had been necessary for starting the business.

Despite this loss of momentum, the economic climate in the post–World War II period was so favorable to the industry that ABP enjoyed record prosperity. The residential, commercial, and industrial building boom that was fueled by demand, pent up during the war, combined with the rapid expansion of industrial and construction markets for plywood to spark a volume explosion. Industry capacity still lagged behind demand, translating into a highly favorable price structure. The net result was an almost uninterrupted progression in sales and earnings for almost a decade. Moreover, ABP had a decided advantage over latecomers in the industry: Those vast timberlands had been acquired long ago, when land and forests were cheap and could be had for the asking, if one knew how to approach the right politicians.

To make the picture ABP presented even more enticing, the company had always been financed in the most conservative manner. Debt was minimal, and no preferred stock had been issued. During the Depression of the 1930s, the shrewd management had employed its cash resources to buy additional land, particularly in Mississippi, and to expand its holdings while other companies were selling property for whatever it would bring, in order to raise cash and avoid going broke.

As if all these virtues weren't sufficient, there was more (which is a little like discovering that Miss America is not only beautiful and charming but has also graduated from the Cordon Bleu School of Cooking with honors and reads and understands Plato). American Building Products' extensive expansion during the thirties had been accomplished almost completely by "internally generated funds"—that is, through cash generated from depletion, depreciation, and retained earnings. There had been no borrowing, no mortgages, no debts.

ABP's dividend policy followed the same conservative, self-contained policy. The company rarely paid out more than a third of its earnings in cash dividends to its shareholders. This meant that during bad times, when other companies were cutting shareholders' returns to the bone, and shareholders were occasionally cutting their throats, ABP was serenely maintaining its dividend rate, and moving it to ever higher levels when earnings went up. To complete this almost unbelievably blissful picture (imagine Miss America having a substantial private income in addition to the other virtues previously mentioned), not only did ABP hold its dividends during lean times, it paid extra ones during more prosperous periods. Payments were currently running at $0.35 quarterly, or a $1.40 annual rate, plus a year-end extra of $0.50 for each of the past two years. Miss America, I love you.

ABP certainly looked like a beautiful, sound operation. I am not quite so cynical that I know the price of everything and the value of nothing, but before proceeding to act, I found it essential to ask myself: What is ABP stock worth?

The proper valuation of stocks is an intricate problem around which a whole art (perhaps necromancy is the more appropriate term) of security analysis has evolved. Historically, yield, which is simply a percentage return to the stock buyer in the form of cash dividends on his or her investment, was the most critical standard for valuing common stocks. In the post–World War II era of ever more confidence in economic growth, the yield factor has become less significant. In periods of rapid economic expansion and generally pervasive optimism, investors tend to appraise stocks on anticipated growth rates. The go-go years of the 1920s and the 1960s featured a conventional wisdom that growth would be sustained indefinitely. The price-earnings ratio became the centerpoint for stock valuation in this climate of optimism, and the loftiness of the appraisal is largely dependent on how sanguine expectations are for future expansion. In such an environment, present yield is largely irrelevant. The critical variable is the valuation applied to a projected stream of dividends, which, of course, will depend upon earning power well into the future.

Now, I've been in this business for decades, and I can't be too emphatic in asserting my belief that price-earnings ratios mean very little. Stock prices are not a cold, rational reflection of current earnings or conditions. They are symptomatic of expectations, fantasies, dreams, fears, anxieties, fashions, and assorted lunacies and irrationalities. Stocks rarely sell where the rationalists say they "should." They are usually either too cheap or too expensive, although the sophistry of Wall Street, with its paradoxical combination of arrogance and justifiably low self-esteem, can always rationalize that the "efficient market" is making a valid valuation.

Stocks usually become even more excessively cheap or dear before they tend to reverse course and cross that mystical level of "fair valuation"—which is where the commentators believe the stock *should* sell in view of its earnings and dividends. But stocks, as inanimate pieces of paper, don't react according to human behavioral principles. The application of the pathetic fallacy, as you will soon discover, is a prevalent occupational disease afflicting professional portfolio managers.

A vital factor in considering stock price changes is that they are as much a function of when as of what, of the prevailing investment fashion as of earnings and dividends, or general business conditions. If, at one particular moment, for whatever reason, too many owners want to sell XYZ, the stock will plummet to a level completely independent of its apparent value. Conversely, unrealistically high prices result from intense urgency to own a stock *now*. Bear in mind that the stock market is an auction market, differing from Parke Bernet only in that it involves numerous sellers as well as buyers. Prices are directly related to the degree of urgency that engulfs its participants.

All of these considerations are highly relevant to the decisions of more rational buyers and sellers, acting quite differently from those motivated by emotion. Compared with industrial stocks in general and with building stocks in particular, ABP stock had always sold at a price that was in a fairly conversative ratio to its earnings. The company had also, as noted, provided shareholders with an above-average yield. The reason for the company's humble and neglected status on Wall Street to date was due in part to the stock's almost complete lack of "sponsorship"—nobody who was anybody in the investment community gave a damn about what price the stock was commanding. Banks, trust companies, and brokerage houses were indifferent to it, since none had a large position in the stock. The company itself was unconcerned, since in recent history it had not been necessary to go to the Street to raise additional funds by issuing new stock or selling bonds. Management, except for the Founder family, had no sizable shareholdings and had not given generous options to buy stock to executives as an incentive for them to remain with the firm. As a consequence, since there was no intention on management's part to sell equity to raise capital or to issue shares in exchange for assets, no one cared whether the stock was high or low. Control rested with the Founder family, and thus a raid on the company was almost impossible.

It is fashionable to condemn so-called raiders. In fact, they epitomize a free market at work, allocating capital to its more efficient use. Often, when a stock sells well below the liquidating or "book" value of its assets, outsiders will attempt to gain control and turn these assets into cash, which could mean a handsome gain indeed. Legislation on the state level to restrict such moves actually serves often to entrench incompetent and occasionally dishonest management. Unfortunately, the American shareholder is generally passive. Rather than attempting to replace bad management in publicly owned companies, the individual, and the institutional shareholder, usually decides to sell his stock position and buy shares in a company with whose stewardship he is more comfortable.

In contrast to ABP's regal indifference to the market valuation of its shares, many companies spend almost as much time and effort advertising the merits of their shares as promoting their products. Popular techniques include the maintenance of large public relations staffs, whose function is to nurture a strong liaison with Wall Street analysts. In return for attention to the stocks of these companies, analysts are provided with confirmation of their earnings estimates and with someone to blame in the event the estimates prove egregiously wrong, a not infrequent occurrence.

Another part of stock promotion technique involves such gimmicks as stock dividends and splits to engender a sense of good feeling in stockholders, who evidently do not realize that the only spendable dividend is cash. This wooing of the Wall Street community produces more confidence in the company among brokerage houses and a greater willingness to recommend a stock to customers or to take an investment position for the brokerage house itself.

When circumstances turn sour and the romance falters due to disappointed expectations, the public relations staff can ameliorate the problem by providing reassuring rationalizations for unpleasant or adverse developments within the company or economic climate. It is important that investors are comfortable owning a stock. The feeling of comfort motivates shareholders to hold on to their investments and not panic in times of slight adversity.

The impact of this attention to public relations by a sophisticated management is significant in determining the demand for, and consequently the price of, a stock. The public relations company's efforts involve nebulous intangibles indeed, but these can be potent in surrounding a stock—and the ownership thereof—with an aura of stability and prestige. This is essential to attract that sponsorship by which a prominent brokerage house or investment firm becomes associated with an issue.

Sponsorship is not a charitable affair. There is benefit on both sides of the transaction. On Wall Street, a sponsor is usually a prominent investment house with a reputation for making money for its clients. The aura of success attracts a substantial and vocal following among large private and institutional investors.

In its more primitive form, sponsorship is provided by the underwriting firm that originally made the first offering of the stock to the public. If you are the owner of a business and you want to sell a part of it to the public, you contract with an underwriter who, for a generous cut, will use his distribution network and experience to sell the stock to public investors. The underwriter is the initial means of educating the investing public to a company's merits, providing introductions for management to important security analysts or portfolio managers. He will also try to enable the "right people" to get in on the ground floor of an expected rise in the price of the stock and attempt to get favorable publicity. His compensation is an initial commission plus handsome fees for handling subsequent financing for the sponsored off-spring.

ABP, however, was a Street orphan with no sponsorship. Management had never made an effort to interest Wall Street in its affairs. Not one brokerage house had undertaken to stimulate enthusiasm for this investment opportunity. ABP plodded along, achieving a reputation for solidity but also dullness. The stockholders were generally satisfied with their investment, judging from the moderate volume of trading and the price stability of the stock over long periods of time. The typical holder was a conservative, unadventurous type who had bought shares for the apparently safe dividend and in the expectation that the company would share in the secular expansion of the building products industry. A few stockholders were probably attracted by ABP's vast square miles of timber-lands, happily combining a touch of wilderness with a hedge against inflation.

I initially became aware of the existence of ABP through a fairly typical Wall Street combination of circumstances. My associate, Confrer, had become a member of the board of directors just after World War II, when our firm had handled a small bond issue for ABP. Underwriting firms frequently place one of their executives on the board of a company as a condition of handling a financing. This allows the underwriter to oversee the progress of the company and to assure first call on future financing business. Although the indebtedness had long ago been paid off, and the bonds redeemed, management was so indifferent to Wall Street that the other directors had never bothered to ask why on earth Confrer was still on the board. Confrer carefully followed company affairs, although he told me he was frequently hard-pressed to keep either eye open at board meetings. Between yawns, Confrer kept me acquainted with ABP's progress.

From what I learned, there was no reason to anticipate any great change in the price of ABP stock. Management was competent, if unaggressive. Founder, Jr., had held the office of chief executive since shortly after the First World War. Now in his late sixties and having developed a zealous devotion to golf, he had moved up to chairman of the board and become a figurehead. Management was in the hands of three rather desiccated vice-presidents in charge of materials, production, and sales.

Though nothing dramatic was happening, and nothing seemed likely to happen soon, it seemed to me inevitable that history, which sweeps the whole world in directions never dreamed of, might just possibly have some small effect on ABP. For the moment, however, this was no capital-gains vehicle for me. The stock was cheap, but not *that* cheap. A situation does not interest me unless there is a good possibility of a 100% return on my investment within a reasonable period, say, two or three years, and unless the maximum risk of loss can be reasonably quantified at 25%. I couldn't see any likelihood of ABP stock doubling in price in the foreseeable future.

Suddenly one day almost two years ago, there were some dramatic changes in the hitherto lethargic affairs of ABP that promised action and excitement. The chairman of the company, Founder, Jr., finally broke par at the country club and in his excitement promptly succumbed to a heart attack. Choosing a successor presented no problem. Founder III had been groomed for the presidency for the past decade and immediately assumed control. All involved sighed with relief and prepared to revert to a comfortable stupor.

But Founder III had his own ideas, being of a more evolved species than Grandpa and Founder, Jr. A degree from Harvard Business School had brought new ideas about how Wall Street worked and about the ingenious ways stock might be used to build and expand a company into new and dazzling areas. Having quietly but impatiently spent years of apprenticeship in the business, hovering respectfully in the background while Founder, Jr., and the comatose vice-presidents droned on at their deadly conferences, he was now eager to take over, to run the company—and the stock—according to his own master plan.

Unlike his predecessors, Founder III viewed the stock market not as "something those lounge-lizard Eastern pansies play with" but rather as an effective means of creating valuable paper that could be used to buy tangible values and build an empire. Founder III had witnessed the evolution of some spectacular entrepreneurial pyramids in the postwar era, and he realized that their expansion was based primarily on exchanging high-priced (relative to earnings, dividends, and book value) stock for real assets and earnings. Through such means as excellent sponsorship and effective public relations, a company could transform its stock into highly prized currency to be used instead of cold cash to buy other concerns.

Onward and upward. The initial step, decided Founder III, was going to be as up-to-date as space travel. His first move was to capitalize on the spectacular vogue for technology stocks by undertaking an acquisition that would make Wall Street wake up and take notice. When Confrer brought me this piece of news, I didn't exactly gloat; I just purred a little. The overture was over, the house lights had dimmed, and it was time for the real drama to begin.

3 The Magic of Street Math

During the gestation period of twiddling his thumbs at board meetings and of sitting on hands that itched to take over the wheel at ABP, Founder III hadn't been completely idle. Matter of fact, for several years he'd been making quite a neat little pile in the stock market with his private funds by the shrewd application of his own sound investment theories —at least that's what he attributed his success to.

Mostly, he'd been just plain lucky. His instincts had led him to invest money in a current stock market vogue—electronics issues. During the period when he made his private pile, hundreds of small electronics concerns had gone public. The vogue was for "technology situations," the mere sound of which had a magical effect on investors, who were practically begging for the privilege of paying astronomical prices for the golden opportunity to join in the infinite growth that promoters' greed and prevailing myths promised for the industry.

This passion for electronics stocks hadn't escaped other crafty corporate managements either. It was a perfect setup for boosting the market valuation of stocks in their own companies. This is done by a neat device which, briefly, goes like this: The Containerized Sanitation Logistics Company, maker of garbage cans, had 1 million shares outstanding and was earning $1 million, or the equivalent of $1 a share. Its stock was selling for, say, $10 a share, or at 10 times earnings, with a total market value of $10 million.

The second company involved in this gambit, Cosmic Transistors Co., which made, of course, transistors, had 200,000 shares outstanding and was earning $200,000, or $1 a share. Its stock was selling at $25 a share, or the luxurious 25 times earnings commanded by investment vehicles enjoying a strong vogue, for a total market valuation of $5 million. Investors at this time were willing to pay 25 times earnings in order to participate in the growth and glamour of Cosmic. So, suppose that Containerized Sanitation acquired Cosmic Transistors, exchanging 500,000 newly issued shares of its own stock, worth $5 million at prevailing market prices, for Cosmic's 200,000 shares. Now, the net result of this marriage would be that the merged companies (let us call the resulting company Containerized Cosmic) had some 1.5 million shares outstanding, with earnings of $1.2 million, or $0.80 a share.

What should Containerized Cosmic sell at? What is it "worth"? Separately, we had Cosmic's 200,000 shares valued at a total of $5 million by the market and Containerized's 1 million shares selling at $10 million. By the alchemy of Wall and Broad streets, the whole was substantially larger than the sum of its parts. The market would not only willingly place the high valuation enjoyed previously by Cosmic alone on the combined earnings but was even willing to pay a premium for the enterprise and genius of a management that had engineered the whole deal. Net result—Containerized Cosmic stock now sold at $24 a share, or 30 times the combined earnings of $0.80 per share, for a total market valuation of the merged concerns of $36 million. Where else but on Wall Street could $5 million plus $10 million equal $36 million?

Furthermore, if Containerized Cosmic was using its noggin, or that of its sophisticated Wall Street bankers, it could now use this inflated paper and buy companies that didn't enjoy such exalted status among the investment community and whose stocks were selling at perhaps 10 times earnings. With its splendid new image, that of an "electronics company applying new technology to consumer markets" (among them, I suppose, transistorized garbage cans?), Wall Street would kindly give the same high valuation to newly acquired earnings regardless of what kind of business they were derived from.

I'm skeptical of the whole concept of the price-earnings ratio as a yardstick of value, but there is no denying its usefulness in motivating purchases or sales when the temperament of speculators demands such rationalization. And there are occasional situations when revaluations made by serious and rational investors can result in dynamic price performance. Dramatic examples of this are the upward valuation of the steel industry in the late 1950s, and the downward revaluation of it in the mid-1960s. Indeed, it can be argued that the downward revaluation of common stocks that dates from the early 1960s is a reasonable readjustment to an economy that has passed its zenith and has entered a postindustrial stage.

Meanwhile, back at the mahogany-paneled Victorian boardroom of ABP, this technique of inflating the value of a company's stock and then using the inflated paper to buy other assets and sources of earnings had not escaped the glazed eye of Founder III. This technique, he felt, was ideal for realizing his objective of building a corporate empire (paging Ozymandias), using plodding old ABP as his base of operations. All he needed was to begin to acquire companies that were enjoying steadily rising appraisals from Wall Street, in the hope that the market would value the company's total earnings at the same lofty price they put on the most highly appraised segment of business. If he timed his purchases shrewdly, he thought, the glamour companies he acquired could be mixed with the occasional purchase of a more prosaic (and more stable) company with substantial assets, at a bargain price, using the inflated value of the paper (*i.e.*, ABP stock) as payment.

For some time before Founder III had ascended the Grand Rapids regal throne of the family business, he'd had his acquisitive eye on the company he intended to use as the first building block in what he hoped would ultimately become a giant financial edifice. It was a small company that manufactured transistors, called Magic Transistors, formed just three years previously by two engineers who had left IBM after working there long enough to learn, from careful observation, exactly how to spot and capitalize quickly on the rapidly obsolescing trends in the burgeoning young transistor industry. They had absorbed all that was to be absorbed from IBM about the most up-to-date techniques in manufacturing and marketing transistors. In just three years the sales volume of their new company had soared from less than a mere $200,000 a year to a respectable $5 million. Competition in the industry was scant and based on technological edge or reliability, not on price, a phenomenon common in new fields. Thus, profit margins were spectacular; even after very generous salaries for the principals and assorted "fringe benefits" were deducted, $0.40 of each dollar in sales was pretax profit.

Just before Magic offered its stock to the public, some ominous signs began to surface and were apparent to friends of mine in the industry. Numerous new competitors were entering the industry, and there were sporadic indications of price competition to gain market share. To offset the adverse impact on profit margins, the two founders of Magic, whom we will call Mr. Marvel and Mr. Engineer, pulled in their belts, tightened up on some of their "expenses," and reduced their salaries. These timely moves reduced total general and administrative expenses in their company by more than $100,000 yearly, which was not insignificant in relation to the actual size of the company. The savings gave the impression that profit margins were widening when, in fact, they were narrowing, and enabled the company to maintain its as yet unbroken string of consecutive annual earnings gains.

When Magic "went public," it was capitalized at 600,000 shares and was earning about $600,000. All had been owned by Marvel and Engineer. They kept 400,000 shares and offered 200,000 shares to public investors at $15 a share, or 15 times the previous year's earnings of $1 and about 12 times the expected profits of the company for the coming year. The stock had scarcity value and the vogue for electronics was red hot so, like a beautiful white bird, the stock promptly shot up to around $40 a share. Not bad, to put it very mildly, considering that this price represented a valuation on the stock of over 50 times the previous year's earnings. It gave the company a market value of $24 million (or almost triple its debut valuation, a rich one at that, of $9 million). The two engineers had each kept 200,000 shares of the company's stock, which meant that their "estates" were now worth $8 million, and they were both drawing salaries of $150,000 a year.

Founder III was very interested indeed in Magic Transistors. He'd met Mr. Marvel and Mr. Engineer at his country club during cocktail hour, that most beautiful time of day (Marvel and Engineer had just joined, sponsored, of course, by the "right people"). The acquaintanceship bloomed, and Founder had, himself, accumulated 15,000 shares of stock —10,000 at the initial offering and 5,000 more immediately afterward on the open market. His 15,000 shares averaged out at a cost of about $18 a share.

The board of directors of ABP stayed awake long enough to approve young Founder's plan to merge with Magic Transistors. All of the board members were either ancient operating personnel or personal friends of the Founder family. Founder III was young, dynamic, and persuasive. The board was well aware that he had done well with his private electronics investments; he had modestly confessed to same. (They were not aware, however, that Founder privately owned 15,000 shares of Magic stock and stood to enjoy a generous personal windfall from the proposed merger plan.) The terms were to be an even exchange of stock—one share of ABP for one share of Magic Transistor. Confrer, still the only "outsider" on the company board, roused himself out of a semi-torpor and sat up—it looked as if something was about to happen at ABP after all.

Now, just before the proposed merger was brought before the board, ABP had been selling at around $38 a share, yielding 5% from the $1.90 total dividend payments per year. Three days before Founder sprang the idea of the merger at the board meeting, ABP stock suddenly attracted a little trading interest and moved up to $42 a share. It seemed as if somebody knew something. The day before the board meeting the stock jumped another 3 points. Guess why. Right you are—Founder III had had a few extra martinis at the club and had let slip to a few friends that a "big merger" was under consideration.

The actual announcement of the merger had the desired effect on the price of ABP stock, though the reaction was a little delayed. Some traders immediately bought on the news, while others who had already bought in anticipation of the merger sold. The result was a slight bulge up in the price to 48, then a retreat back down to the low 40s.

A few days later, the financial sections of leading newspapers and the *Wall Street Journal* carried stories on the merger and quoted Founder III to the effect that "the acquisition of Magic Transistors by ABP represented the first step in a major program of diversification into the more rapidly growing segments of the economy." In addition, this dynamic executive indicated that additional expansion moves were under consideration. Moreover, he projected that ABP income for the year would reach a record high.

This rich prose was traceable directly to the public relations firm of Segam, Inc., which Founder III had just hired to ease the upward path to Glamourville for his stodgy old company. What the news releases assiduously avoided mentioning was any reference to per-share earnings, since the acquisition of Magic Transistors had resulted in considerable dilution of share earnings. While total profits would reach a record, whether profits *per share* on the larger number outstanding would make a parallel increase was another matter.

Responsive as a geisha girl, the stock now reacted with a bang. It was already at a high for the year, and up it spurted to 55, a *historic* high. It was moving easily now, since there was no overhead supply, a term referring to turnover of stock at a higher price level at a previous time. If, for example, stock once sold at 50 and is *now* selling at 40, one can say there is an overhead supply, which represents stock bought at higher prices held by now disenchanted investors, speculators, or traders waiting to "get even"; such are prone to offer their stock for sale once it again climbs back up to what they originally paid for it. But ABP's supply-demand situation was strong; everyone who owned the stock had a paper profit. There was no chance of a vendetta by unhappy holders waiting to get out even.

Now let us see how the acquisition of Magic Transistors had inflated the paper value of ABP stock. Before the acquisition, ABP was earning $6 million, or the equivalent of $4 for each of its 1.5 million shares. The stock was selling at $40 per share, for a total market valuation for the company of $60 million. Magic, with 600,000 shares outstanding (of which 400,000 were owned by the two founders) was earning

$600,000, or $1 per share, and was valued by the market at $40 per share, or $24 million. Total earnings of the two companies were $6.6 million; market valuation $84 million.

After the acquisition, ABP had 2.1 million shares outstanding (the original 1.5 million plus the 600,000 exchanged for Magic shares), and was earning $6.6 million, or $3.14 a share. The market wasn't quite willing to give the whole package the same valuation it had accorded Magic, but at 55 the stock was selling at about 17 times earnings and the whole company had a market valuation of $115.5 million. By the simple act of merger, $24 million + $60 million became $115.5 million—an additional $31.5 million in paper value had been created. More Wall Street magic numbers!

Selling after the merger at 55, was ABP stock overpriced or underpriced? It was probably overpriced, but there wasn't any indication whether it would now get cheaper or become more expensive.

4 An Ancient

Trading Device

Founder III quickly began to capitalize upon an investing public infatuated with electronics and immediately announced a major expansion program for Magic. A new $3 million plant that already had been on Magic's drawing boards was to be built, and the electronics line was to be extended "into other fields where our technological skills can be best utilized." Magic until now had gotten along with leased facilities, valued around $500,000.

One would assume that the substantial capital outlay announced for new facilities was part of a deliberate and carefully planned expansion program. This conclusion naturally follows from one of the myths of the contemporary business scene. Professional corporate managers are as a matter of course attributed foresight and intelligence in their management of capital. Their advancement to important managerial positions alone creates an almost unrebuttable presumption of expertness. But too frequently political flair rather than management talent is the key to advancement in large cor-

27

porations, so manipulative, not managerial, skills become critical.

Most huge companies have sufficient momentum so that, like the nation, they can survive incompetence at the top for an amazingly long time. This prevalent myth of corporate infallibility is one of the main elements contributing to the consummate passivity of the American shareholder, and the disastrous postwar experience of a Montgomery Ward or a Chrysler or a Penn Central has done surprisingly little to destroy it.

I had been tempted to sell short ABP stock after its run-up on the acquisition of Magic, as I felt the stock had probably become overvalued at 50, but years of experience on Wall Street have taught me never to underestimate the buying frenzy of the speculating public once some particular fancy —or fantasy—has caught on and is proving profitable. ABP could well continue its upward trend, for stocks rarely sell for what they are "worth" by analytical standards. They are either déclassé, unreasonably cheap, and likely to get cheaper, or in vogue, excessively dear, and likely to get more expensive until the vogue exhausts itself. ABP was selling at its highest appraisal in terms of earnings in memory and providing its lowest yield, yet there were no signs that the demand for stock would be met except at higher prices.

Short selling is an ancient trading device, dating all the way back to biblical times, when Esau shorted his inheritance, which he had not yet received from Isaac, by selling it to his brother Jacob for a bowl of soup. He sold something he didn't have but expected to obtain later. The same type of transaction takes place with stocks. The short seller makes a sale of ABP shares that he does not yet own. His broker borrows the ABP shares from an actual stockholder and delivers them to the buyer. The short seller, expecting the stock to decline, plans to actually buy ABP shares later on at a lower price and deliver them back to the lender, realizing a profit from the difference between the selling price and the purchase price.

In order to prevent manipulators from purposely driving stock prices down through short sales (this was prevalent during the 1920s), the practice is regulated: You can sell only on an uptick. For example, if XYZ is selling at 65, then goes down to 64½, a short sale on the Exchange floor can be made on the next transaction only if it is higher than 64½.

The news of the Magic expansion program having had the desired impact, ABP's stock shot up to around 60 and held there for some weeks. Trading volume had now soared to around 50,000 shares a week, more than 10 times the average of recent years. A large number of longtime shareholders who had bought and held the stock for income no longer found it suitable for their purposes. They sold largely to short-term speculators and traders who, in turn, were willing to sell or buy on a few points' mark-up or concession. The floating supply of the stock (the number of shares not locked up in the hands of long-term investors) had perhaps tripled, but it was probably still less than one-quarter of the total outstanding. More of these new holders were willing to trade in and out of the situation, however, making for generally greater liquidity for the stock and, thus, for higher daily turnover.

The stock began to act a litle sloppy around 60 in the following weeks. One could feel that the sense of urgency to own the stock had peaked. It seemed that virtually everyone anxious to own ABP shares had taken his position, and, as an old Wall Street adage goes, it takes buying to put stocks up but they fall of their own weight. ABP had begun to sag gently toward the middle 50s when the financial community was greeted by another announcement, just three weeks after the Magic expansion plan.

The company had just purchased, for cash, a small botanical research firm concentrating on tree farming and experimenting with means of accelerating plant growth. Simultaneously, ABP announced plans to build a vast new research center to highlight the new corporate concept of "tomorrow's product from today's research."

This news release was widely disseminated, together with reiteration that net income for the year would reach an all-time high. Management had again, of course, failed to make any allusion to share profits, for, due to the larger number outstanding and the dilution from Magic, share profits would actually show a substantial decline.

The news was followed by a quick run-up by the stock, but this time on somewhat less volume than that which had accompanied previous advances to new peaks. When ABP moved into the middle 70s there was a sudden raft of rumors that the recently acquired research company had developed a technique for accelerating the growth of timber. Food for fantasy indeed! ABP would be able to grow trees twice as fast as anyone else in the industry and consequently enjoy an unmatchable competitive advantage!

The first indication of possible trouble was the announcement of a large secondary distribution in the stock just six months after the Magic acquisition. This is a technique used on Wall Street to market a sizable block of stock after the primary distribution (such as that by Magic Transistor of 200,000 shares initially to the public) has taken place. After all, if owners of a few hundred thousand shares were suddenly to give their brokers orders to sell "at the market," chaos would result. Instead, a number of brokerage houses join to distribute these holdings to their customers at a set price, usually determined by prevailing market quotations at the time the secondary distribution takes place.

The offering was to be of 400,000 shares of ABP, a figure matching the combined holdings of Marvel and Engineer. I quickly learned that they were the sellers. Why were they unloading? For good reasons: New entrants into the transistor field were multiplying like rabbits. The practice of cutting prices in order to gain a share of the market was becoming commonplace. Technological improvements in production were rapidly reducing manufacturing costs—but not as rapidly as prices were declining. A glance at a representative group of transistor stocks showed that virtually all were down from their highs, a phenomenon attributed by most glib market commentators to "profit taking."

The secondary was timed beautifully, however, and was gotten off at around 65—where the stock had retreated on news of the impending offering. Interestingly, of the 400,000 shares offered, two large blocks (one of 100,000 shares, the other 50,000) were taken by two prominent mutual funds, which apparently wanted to get on the science bandwagon but weren't quite daring enough to buy one of the exclusively electronics outfits selling at 30 or so times earnings. Moreover, the fund managers were afraid this might be their last chance to get a large position in ABP stock without having to run prices up through open market purchases. These blocks were much later to be key elements in my program to amass a large position in the stock.

ABP now began to look like an attractive short sale, but once again I preferred to short it at a lower price. By the same token, I am often willing to wait and pay up for a stock after I feel greater assurance that a further rise will follow and that the probability of making a profit is greater, although the amount of gain would be smaller. I viewed the fundamental situation, *i.e.*, the outlook for the company's business, as deteriorating, but thus far there were no definitive signs that the technical position of the stock—essentially the supply-demand balance—had turned unfavorable.

The secondary had gone off well at 65 and the stock had immediately bounced back up to just above 70—within a point or so of its all-time high. One of the basic elements in the supply-demand situation that can set off an important decline is the existence of unhappy holders of a stock. With ABP within striking distance of its all-time high, the vast majority of shareholders had a profit and, accordingly, could be presumed to be happy with their ownership and have no incentive to sell, particularly since there were as yet no signs that ABP was anything but flourishing.

In the following weeks, the electronics stocks generally began to ease a bit. Apparently industry insiders had become well aware of the deteriorating price situation in transistors and were unloading, but at a gradual pace—dumping stock in a hurry would have ruined their own markets. ABP now dipped back to around 66. I decided the time was ripe to let out a line of shorts.

My basic thinking at 66 was this: Most important, I was sure I was dealing with a deteriorating business situation. The unanswered question was whether there would be a sufficiently strong vogue for the stock so that, despite the worsening profit outlook, there would be another sharp run up and, for me, a whipsaw. I thought not. From what I knew of the situation, the buyers, whether individual speculators or professional portfolio managers, were simply riding a fad. Regardless of what you may feel about the merits of mutual funds as a means of hiring professional management by the small investor, my own experience with fund portfolio managers is that they are no better or worse than the average brokerage house analyst. They are not infallible and are vulnerable to the same psychological disabilities in their market operations as anyone else. To their credit, however, many funds, unlike individuals who made similar mistakes, are willing to admit their errors quickly and take a loss on the first indication that something is wrong.

My strategy was this: If I could force the funds to reexamine their commitments, they would stop supporting the stock by their buying. They might even offer their large holdings on the market, substantially accelerating and telescoping what I considered an inevitable substantial decline.

ABP was finding sufficient buyers to hold the price at around 66, but I considered these buyers irrational and imprudent. Most were probably impelled by the "down from the high" lure: The stock is now 66, it used to be 72, therefore it is a bargain. Others, remembering the secondary offering, felt the stock would attract support from the underwriters, bringing about a rally from this area.

Most important of all, there was now what we call overhead supply in the stock. There had been a substantial turnover in the past few weeks above 66—and all of these holders represented potential sources of offerings if the stock were to rally, thus aborting any advance. Moreover, they might well panic at some point after a serious decline set in and their losses began to grow. For the stock to move up and go through this overhead supply area would require time and heavy volume, the two requirements that would allow me to reverse my short position with a minimum loss if I believed my strategy wrong.

I began to sell short the stock in the 66–68 area. Turnover in the issue continued to total about 5,000 shares a day. I was unable to short in blocks of more than 300 shares at a time. There were obviously no large bidders for the stock, only scattered small buyers. And of course my shorting helped to keep the stock price from rising, since I was adding to the supply.

In a matter of a few weeks, I had established a short position of about 15,000 shares of ABP in the 66–68 area, and now the stock slipped back to 65, the price at which the secondary had been sold some weeks before. The stock had receded to 65 a number of times previously and bounced back to slightly above that level. It was apparent that there was a large bidder absorbing stock at 65.

I had two alternative methods of breaking the stock. I could put in a large offering at 65⅛, in effect saturating the demand for the stock and putting a lid on the price. The net result would have been to force the bidder at 65 to absorb all of the stock put on the market for sale. The failure of ABP stock to advance—being held back by my offering of shorts at 65⅛—would attract sellers and increase the pressure of supply on the bidder. The bidder, however, if sophisticated, could see that a possible bear raid (a determined attempt to force the stock down) was developing and could attempt to outsmart me by bidding for tens of thousands of shares at 65⅛, forcing me to overextend my short position. Then, through buying quickly, the bidder could mark the stock up —let's say to 70—attracting boardroom scalpers and other traders, resulting in a move to a new high. And I could not break the price by dumping stock on and saturating the bidder, since I did not own any stock and could only short on an uptick.

The alternative method open to me was to attempt to knock the stock down in the over-the-counter market, expecting this to lead to a break on the Exchange. When a listed stock becomes extremely active and develops a large following, many over-the-counter dealers begin to make a market in it. This had happened with ABP products. The over-the-counter spread between bid and asked price was somewhat broader, usually runing to ¾ or a full point. Now it was 64½ bid–65½ offered; it was obvious that the o-t-c dealers sensed a possible decline and were trying to protect themselves by a wide spread. I could short stock over the counter without an uptick and I could sell it below the 65 level.

I immediately began to offer a few 300-share lots at 64½ to the two largest dealers in the o-t-c market who were trading the stock. A few minutes after each sale, there were ticks (printed ticker transactions) on the Exchange of 300 shares each at 65—the o-t-c dealers were selling on the Exchange floor the stock they had bought from me. More offerings at 65 began to come across the tape, for just as strength attracts buying, weakness attracts selling. I now offered 2,000 shares to one o-t-c dealer at 64½. He would take only 400 at that price and dropped the quote to 64 bid-65½ offered. I hit his bid, but he would take only 100 shares. I immediately went to a second major o-t-c dealer and offered him 1,000 shares at 64½; he hadn't yet had time to change his quote. He would take only 100 shares at 64½ and dropped his market to 63½–65½. Obviously he was in immediate contact with the other important o-t-c house and realized that offerings of stock were accelerating.

A few minutes later, there were sales of 1,500 shares and 1,200 shares at 65 on the Stock Exchange ticker tape. It was apparent that the o-t-c houses were unloading their own inventory of ABP shares, not just what they had bought from me. I felt now that it was only a matter of time before a cascade of selling would begin. Moments later, there were a few prints of 200, 300, and 800 shares of ABP at 65, interspersed by a few 100-share lots at the same price. For a moment, I was anxious. How large a basket was under the stock at 65? Perhaps there was someone who knew something I didn't about the situation that made him so anxious to buy the stock. However, he obviously wasn't anxious enough to bid up for shares and, from my analysis, he wasn't a smart buyer. If he would just let the stock break below 65, the 400,000 shares bought at the secondary would show a paper loss and he could buy all the stock he wanted at lower prices—he would trigger trend followers and traders into selling, thus creating bargains for himself.

I had timed my sales for late morning around eleven-thirty, hoping that offerings would accelerate during the lunch hour, when many speculators and self-styled tape readers walk into boardrooms. By one o'clock my advertising campaign, the slogan of which was "ABP is going down—sell me," had been a success. The tens of thousands of people in boardrooms throughout the country had seen that message spelled out as clearly on the ticker tape as it would be to someone in Times

Square watching the illustrated transmission at the top of the Allied Chemical Building. After about 7,000 shares had gone through at 65, the next ticks were 600 at 64½, 2,000 at 64, 700 at 63¾, 500 at 63½, 200 at 63, 700 at 62¾. The stock hit a low of 61 in late afternoon, rallying to 62¼ by the close.

What had happened to make my campaign a success is that a lot of stop-loss orders had been set off at 65 and below. A stop-loss is a standing order to buy at a price above the current market or sell at a price below it. Such orders are frequently placed by traders to protect unrealized profits or to limit losses. They are a self-disciplining device, triggered automatically when a transaction occurs at the specified price. A few bargain hunters had sparked ABP's slight recovery at the close.

In the next few days the stock fell to around 56, after holding briefly at 60 while some round-number orders were filled. A typical phenomenon on Wall Street is the public's fancy for round numbers. Small speculators will often place an order to buy or to sell at such numbers as 25, 30, *et cetera*.

I now had a fair unrealized profit on my short position and felt that, with an adverse supply-demand balance and a deteriorating fundamental business situation, I would stay with my short position until there was some reason, either by the action of the stock or from a change in the operating outlook at ABP, to revise my strategy. Little did I realize then how much of a decline in price was ahead for ABP common shares.

5 Black Magic

I now had a sizable short position in ABP (some 40,000 shares sold at an average price of 65), and the technical position of the stock had deteriorated drastically. (The term "technical" refers simply to the supply-demand picture, regardless of the fundamentals, *i.e.*, what is actually happening to the business and assets underlying the piece of paper that represents a share of ABP.) There was now a large amount of stock that would probably be offered for sale on the market if the price rallied, representing purchases by short-term speculators who had bought the stock on the run, figuring they would throw it out in a matter of days with a sizable profit. According to the cynics on Wall Street, an investment is a speculation that went sour. There were now many involuntary "investors" in ABP who would be happy to "get out even" if and when the stock once again reached the price they had paid for it.

The fundamental situation at ABP was also worsening rapidly. The price structure in transistors had collapsed. The larger electronics companies with broader product lines could survive. They continued to make and sell transistors at a loss that was offset by profits from their other product lines. Managements began to realize this was a shake-out period, during which the marginal producers would either go to the wall or be merged with larger companies. Ultimately, and ultimately might mean a long time and after heavy losses, the industry would settle down in the hands of a smaller number of large, efficient producers with some semblance of price leadership provided by the majors. The industry was simply going through normal growing pains—painful indeed for Magic and ABP.

The larger concerns also had other advantages over a simple component maker like Magic. Transistors are just one item used in electronic assemblies and equipment. The big companies could price their complete assemblies at a profitable level, as a loss on one component was more than offset by a profit on another. In addition, more modern equipment and larger volume provided them with a competitive edge.

Magic now found itself losing money, based on the direct costs of labor and materials that went into each transistor unit, before allowing for the cost of other overhead or indirect expenses such as rent, sales and administration costs, and depreciation. The sparkling new $3 million plant was idle, and because of losses on a direct-costs basis, there was no incentive even to continue production. In addition, maintenance charges were running close to $50,000 a month. As the final horror, it had earlier been thought that since the industry was booming, Magic's smaller leased plant would be sublet without difficulty, perhaps even at a profit, to other prospering component companies—but now there were no takers.

Magic had become simply another inefficient, uncompetitive maker of a mass-produced item. It was transistors, but it could have been shoes, tires, ashtrays, whatever. Being neither a particularly low-cost maker nor one that enjoyed captive markets for its output, Magic as it was presently structured was doomed. The losses from Magic's operations mounted, aggravated by the additional burden of overhead on the new plant. This plant had been financed completely from ABP's working capital. Founder III had believed that through accelerated depreciation and the high operating profits projected from the new facility, the investment would be quickly returned.

The situation in the transistor industry was known to many investors. All one had to do was read the trade journals. ABP stock began a gradual but persistent decline, retreating back to the 40 level, at which price it was fairly valued on the normal earning power of building operations and on its dividend payments. And the management of ABP was now faced with a difficult problem. None of the available alternatives was pleasant.

One alternative would be an enormous infusion of additional capital into Magic. The outlays would be directed toward broadening and diversifying Magic's operations in the electronics field, and toward improving manufacturing efficiency by large commitments to new machinery. The program would also entail ambitious and expensive product development. In essence, this alternative was to undertake the creation of a viable factor in the electronics components industry, using as the basic building block a marginal operation thin on management, capital, and product line. Illusions about the genius of Magic's management had evaporated with its profits. The unavoidable inference was that there were no unusual talents in Magic. The organizers had just hit it lucky, like thousands of other electrical engineers at the early stage of the boom in transistors. Marvel and Engineer's genius was limited to timing, from the founding of their transistor business to the selling of their ABP stock.

Another alternative was to cut back Magic's operations in hope of locating a limited but profitable niche in the industry. This seemed impractical for a number of reasons. For one, it was unlikely that Magic could make money as a small producer of a commodity component, or by competing against larger companies enjoying a decisive technological edge. Even had that been possible, there was little point in maintaining a marginally profitable operation, now viewed as completely unrelated to the building products field and having no future.

The final alternative, and the only feasible one, was to dispose of the Magic operation entirely. This would be difficult and would entail substantial losses; ABP had drastically overpaid for Magic, and now there was little allure in this business for any potential buyer. The attributes of this pariah included a product line that was not proprietary and not profitable; a leasehold on a moderately efficient plant, but one that could not now be easily sublet; working capital of about $3 million that included possibly obsolete inventory; and a new $3 million plant that was a constant drain and completely unnecessary to the current operations of the company.

To find a buyer for all this would not be easy, and would surely involve a "distress price," *i.e.*, a loss. The situation, however, had not escaped the notice of professional "finders" —this breed of intermediary acts as a corporate matchmaker. Most of the captive breed operate through brokerage or investment firms that have their own new business departments, an important function of which is to arrange marriages among companies. ABP was approached by Joe Lucanus, one of the shrewder of the free-lance finders.

Lucanus's reputation was that of a pragmatic, aggressive operator who dealt with the more difficult placements. His less gracious competitors called him the "kennel locator for dogs." Lucanus immediately saw the problem in terms of too much plant and investment by Magic and too little business. The transistor line would complement that of an integrated manufacturer, and absorption of Magic would make sense if its large new production facility could be utilized in manufacturing other electronic components.

Magic could also be of interest to a company with a proprietary line that was embarrassingly profitable. Some companies in such an enviable position often diversify into less lucrative areas, hoping thereby to conceal the large margins from their exclusive products. The effect is to discourage com-

petition while simultaneously avoiding the danger of antago-
nizing customers by flaunting the companies' excessive profit
margins.

The search for a buyer was difficult, as the unhappy board
of ABP was continually reminded, but Lucanus finally did
find one who proved a tough bargainer. The price to be paid
to ABP was 50% of inventory valuation, 100% of cash and
receivables, and nothing for goodwill or for going business
value. The price of the new plant was to be $3 million, but
ABP had to take a promissory note at 3% interest, with no
amortization and payable at the end of five years. Even before
discounting the promissory note to its market value, the total
consideration for the Magic subsidiary was to be about $6
million, a whopping loss from the $24 million in market
value of ABP stock that had been paid just a little over a year
ago, not to mention the $3 million subsequently spent for the
new plant.

The negotiations for the sale of Magic took time. During
these months the operating losses from Magic leaped to an
annual rate of over a million dollars. In such circumstances,
when there is a basically nonrecurring problem that is hurt-
ing the parent company and steps are being taken to eliminate
the drain, one might think it would occasion candor by management with its stockholders. The typical reaction, however,
is just the opposite.

Instead of explaining the situation to stockholders and to
the financial community, the management, and particularly
Founder III, clammed up completely. In contrast to the
steady stream of sanguine forecasts and effusive optimism
that had accompanied the acquisitions of Magic and the small
chemical research company, there was now no information
available to the financial community.

As the stock sagged to the 40s, however, management finally felt compelled to issue a statement: "It is necessary to
alter our earnings projections. While the building products

business remains satisfactory [actually profits from this business had risen], severe competitive conditions are having an adverse impact at the present on returns from the Magic subsidiary [which was, of course, losing money] although long-range potentials for growth in the electronics field remain promising." There was no breakdown of results and no clear insight provided into the situation. Although everyone familiar with the transistor industry knew that Magic was heavily in the red, stockholders in general were in the dark. ABP shares were fast losing friends in the Street.

The stock receded further on this news release that raised more questions than it answered, and then fell sharply when the annual report revealed that earnings for the full year had declined to $1 a share. That figure indicated that there was an actual operating loss in the final quarter. The last three months of the year had been seasonally slow for the company's major lines, and Magic's losses were rising. The sharp decline in earnings created doubt whether the dividend would be maintained.

The negotiations to sell the Magic subsidiary dragged on. The buyer was in no hurry, since there was no reason to believe the operation would become more valuable, and the losses mounted. The once serene corporate offices of APB were pervaded with a sense of uneasiness and anxiety that percolated down from the top management. Founder III became increasingly apprehensive. ABP was now in the red on a combined (with Magic) basis—something that hadn't happened even in the days of the Depression—and he was fearful that the Magic subsidiary would never be sold. Remorse about his role in the Magic acquisition compounded his anxiety.

My campaign was about to enter a second phase. I was soon to shift my strategy completely. I would realize my profits on the short position I had established and then begin to look at ABP from the opposite angle, as a potentially profitable investment.

6 Retrenchment

and Disillusion

ABP's working capital position, although still strong relative to most comparable concerns, had deteriorated markedly, thanks to the expansion outlays at Magic and to the buildup of inventories of progressively more doubtful value. Panic seized Founder III and triggered him into two imprudent moves, both of which were to have a stunning impact on the stock. The first was to bring pressure on the board of directors to reduce the dividend, and the second was a rash step aimed at immediately bolstering the working capital position.

The company's total timber holdings were 300,000 acres, most of which had been acquired before World War I, when prices were a fraction of those today. Included in ABP's holdings was a timber tract of 2,100 acres of Michigan lakefront property. In the last two decades this area had become a popular resort; land values had skyrocketed and were still rising. The company was offered $10,000 an acre for land that had been bought for well under a tenth of that price fifty years before. This particular parcel was no longer needed in

operations and had been held as an investment. So Founder
III accepted the offer, receiving $21 million, of which almost
$19 million was a capital gain.

The board had no difficulty in coming to agreement about
the dividend reduction. The board was composed mostly of
conservative, old-line businessmen who felt it was immoral to
pay out dividends that were not being earned from operations.
The long-standing dividend policy of the company was a
conservative one, raising payouts only when there was confidence that a later reduction would not be necessary. Com-
pounding their innate frugality, most directors owned very
few shares of the company stock and were indifferent to the
market's reaction to such a move. Their fiscal conservatism
was also bolstered by the argument that the "company must
live within its means," and the dividend reduction was agreed
upon.

The question now was how much of a reduction: Continuing losses from operations and the protracted and as yet unsuccessful negotiations to sell Magic suggested to some members that a complete omission of dividends was warranted.
Here, however, Confrer's knowledge of the investment community proved useful and prevented an irreparable mistake.
Many institutional investors, such as insurance companies and
noninsured pension plans, are restricted by state law as to
which kinds of common stocks they may include in their
portfolios. A typical requirement is that a common stock
must have paid a cash dividend for a minimum number of
years before it can qualify for purchase by such regulated
institutions. Thus, complete elimination of cash dividends
would raise the possibility of extensive liquidation of holdings by institutional holders, and it would prevent ABP stock
from attracting institutional buyers at a later date when the
situation had improved.

I was extremely anxious that at least a token dividend be
paid, for I sought insurance that when the time arrived to

interest potential buyers in the stock, as many as possible would be eligible to purchase shares. Confrer argued before the board that ABP had an unbroken dividend record for forty years, was still financially sound, would have a strengthened cash position from the sale of the Michigan property, and that, at least as a token of faith in the future, some dividend should be paid. But he recommended a severe reduction, to $0.10 quarterly.

His advice was accepted. The reduction was no great surprise to Wall Street, although the size of it created ambiguity. Some had thought in terms of a decrease from $0.35 to $0.25 quarterly. The $0.10 rate raised more questions than it answered. Was the company making only a token payment because it was actually in no financial position to pay dividends at all? Perhaps the situation could still worsen, and a complete omission of payments would follow. The impact was that owners of the stock were still anxious and unsure whether the worst was behind. A chastened management offered no hope that before too long only good news would be forthcoming.

The stock, having already fallen to the mid-30s in anticipation of a dividend cut, was now under renewed pressure in response to the size of the reduction. ABP sank quickly to 30. A few shorts bought stock to close out their positions and a small rally ensued as bargain hunters, once again lured by the "down from its high" syndrome, were motivated to buy. Trading once again turned dull, and the shares began a slow but relentless slippage.

On the next stage of the decline, volume began to diminish. Most of the more disenchanted small holders of the stock had sold by now. Under these propitious market conditions, I decided to start closing out my short position. I had shorted 40,000 shares in the mid-60s and now, less than nine months later, began to buy in around 1,000 shares a day at prices in the mid-20s. There was no real competition for the shares, and

I was able to cover my whole position in a space of two months —realizing a profit of slightly over $1.5 million on an initial outlay of $2.6 million made only *six* months earlier.

Stage one was now completed. Through Confrer, I had become progressively more familiar with ABP. The short-sale caper had generously compensated me and my clients for my efforts and had given me insight into the trading personality of ABP stock. My plans for the future involved a substantially larger commitment, this time as an investor.

During this period, ABP quarterly reports revealed a continuing sharp contraction in profits. The gain from the sale of the Michigan real estate was noted but not explained. No details were provided to shareholders. It was described simply as a special gain, and the proceeds were credited to the surplus account rather than flowing through the earnings statement. In fact, the disposal of the unspecified asset was regarded by many with more suspicion than optimism. The bias now was naturally against management, and some saw in the sale such desperation to raise cash that vital assets were being liquidated, a policy that would ultimately have an adverse effect on operations.

With share prices declining, earnings contracting, and the dividend shaky, ABP common stock now became a natural candidate for inclusion in Wall Street's "switch lists." The same brokerage houses that less than a year earlier and at triple the current price had considered ABP "a promising growth commitment" now saw it as a suitable candidate for sale in order to obtain funds to switch into more promising situations.

Brokerage houses are well aware that individual stockholders basically don't like to sell their shares and don't want to be told to sell. After all, stock ownership is the raw material of dreams; even in the absence of cash dividends, it offers peripheral rewards. With that magic talisman of the stock certificate, imprinted so austerely by the American Banknote Company, comes an Aladdin's lamp that conjures up pride of ownership in a share of America and participation in a substantial business enterprise without more effort than signing a check on purchase of the shares. How easily one can become an entrepreneur—with two flicks of the wrist: one to dial your broker to buy the stock, the other to write him a check.

But now there were no peripheral felicities accompanying ABP share ownership. Cash dividends were minimal and the once glamorous Magic had become a financial leper. Rather than conjuring up dreams of limitless growth and prosperity, ownership was associated with nightmares of snowballing losses and visions of receivership. ABP, the spawner of this despair, now had no friends, and the brokerage houses risked alienating no one by suggesting a switch.

The "switch list" is a delightful compendium of Wall Street euphemisms. No stocks are ever bad or unattractive; they are just less good and less promising than others. You never sell the dogs in your list, you "upgrade your portfolio." You never take your licking, you just share the custom of the affluent by creating a valuable tax loss.

Behind the general avoidance of sell advice is the realization that if Fleeced Doe doesn't own XYZ stock, and is not disposed to go short, he isn't interested in such advice. If he does own XYZ, he is already sufficiently unhappy without having his misery exacerbated by seeing his mistake assume the authority of a professional sell advice. A "paper loss" is endurable since it is only on paper. (The converse somehow does not seem to be true: Paper profits produce endless joys although they too are "only on paper" and not yet realized.) By this devious definition of reality, a loss becomes a loss by the deus ex machina of a sell confirmation from the broker; until then it is apparently no affront to reason to distinguish it as being "only on paper."

As any veteran of this game has learned from expensive and bitter experience, a key to success in the stock market is a willingness to admit a mistake and to admit it early. The realist who considers stocks as pieces of paper bought for the specific purpose of resale at a higher price is never "locked into" a stock because it shows a loss. Who has the key to the lock anyway? A loss is a loss is a loss.

In contrast to a few years ago, when the boardrooms resounded with the chortles of scalpers who allegedly had bought ABP much lower and had a dozen or so points' profit (on paper), now the only response evoked by a few hundred shares of ABP going across the Trans-Lux was, "That dog!" or a refusal to admit recognition of the ticker symbol. A few months previously, it seemed that everyone in the world owned ABP and, by implication, enjoyed unrealized profits; now no one had ever heard of it.

A few masochists savored their ownership, gaining some psychic rewards. They could boast that they now had a tax loss, the unavoidable implication being that their profits were so large that an offset was desirable—an ingenious rationalization, but a ridiculous one. A loss is never desirable per se. Many Wall Street professionals will go into highly risky situations late in the year if they have already realized large short-term capital gains, since they calculate that Uncle Sam will have to underwrite at least half their losses. But no sane investor would ever willingly enter a situation expecting to lose money.

With ABP now friendless and the worst of the news behind, the time for me to start amassing a position in the stock was rapidly approaching. True, earnings were still declining, entirely because of the Magic losses, and another dividend cut was still possible. But there was every indication that Magic would ultimately be disposed of. If worse came to worst, the operation could simply be dismantled, entailing an enormous —but nonrecurring—loss that would lay the groundwork for a strong recovery in earnings.

Confrer advised me that negotiations for the sale of Magic were proceeding slowly but steadily. My problem was to assess the probable impact of its ultimate disposal on the market. While disposal of Magic would obviously be a plus for the company, perhaps it would not be for the stock. Although in the long run, the stock market has a way of adjusting fairly rationally to the realities of business and the economy, you can never assume that its immediate response will be quite so reasonable. The sale of the Magic subsidiary was subject to different interpretations. The difficulties in the transistor field and the fact that Magic was deeply in the red were now widely known. So the rational response to the disposition of Magic would be the recognition that a drain on ABP had been eliminated and that, subsequently, there would be no dilution of the substantial and gradually growing profits of the building products business.

The negative interpretation would be that the sale of Magic meant that ABP was losing its most promising business, the one with the dynamic future. If Magic was profitable, then the building materials business was not so lucrative and ABP was disposing of an important earning asset. If Magic was unprofitable, its disposal must be at distress prices, resulting in a large loss and a reduction in the total assets of ABP. From a market standpoint, the glamour element would disappear and the valuation of remaining earnings—those from the building products business—would be conservative. The sale of Magic might provide a convenient excuse for wavering sellers to unload their stock. After all, in their investment wisdom they had bought ABP for the potentials of Magic. If that operation were disposed of, *they* would be making no mistake to sell. It would be management's error to have sold Magic.

My conclusion was that the sale of Magic would probably flush out a little more stock. More important, there was no reason to think it would cause a stampede to buy ABP, a consequence that would not suit my purposes. I wanted a situation conducive to competition among sellers, not among buyers. The key to being able to sell or buy in large quantities at your price is having the competition on the other side. If everyone wants to buy ABP, you'll have to pay up for it. If no one else wants it, you can almost name your own price.

I intended to amass over 100,000 shares of ABP, preferably in the $20-a-share area. I felt I would enjoy a period of perhaps three months now before there would be any significant good news coming out of the company. And the year-end tax-selling period would fall within this time. A primary problem was amassing my position in the stock without alerting others to what was going on. There would be time enough, later on, to inform the world of the merits of ABP.

7 Amassing

a Position

A key element in the success of any campaign in the stock market, indeed of any business venture, is the competition's size and degree of sophistication. This is true whether you are buying a large amount of stock or unloading a major position. If the competition is among the buyers and you have the selling side to yourself, you can virtually determine trading levels. The same is true if there are numerous holders of stock anxious to get out and you are the only substantial buyer. Such is essentially what makes runaway markets, either up or down: Panic declines are nothing more than extreme competition among sellers. Urgency determines the momentum and direction of prices.

Always one must remember that the stock market is an auction. Prices depend on the intensity of competing bidders' and sellers' preference to have either stocks or cash. As in all auctions, there are occasionally some remarkable bargains. Too often, however, bidders get carried away by mercantile fever and impulsively pay more than they would under less

51

animated conditions. A vital key to my success, therefore, was limiting competition from other buyers during my campaign to amass a position in ABP stock. The number of persons who would be privy to my campaign—and the reasons behind it—had to be kept at a minimum.

In Wall Street there is a geometric progression among informants. A tells B, who tells C and D, and immediately a secret is in the public domain. You would naturally assume that someone on the inside of a good thing would keep it to himself. But, contrary to what the cynics contend, greed is not the primary motivation on Wall Street—it often takes a back seat to other appetites. The desire to gratify vanity by claiming identification with a knowledgeable "inside" group impels the participant in a campaign to act in a way that makes its objectives unattainable. If everyone were to be let in on the merits of ABP, the price of the stock would instantly soar and I would be unable to establish my position at bargain prices. Later on in my campaign, the desire to be "in" would figure prominently in creating a strong demand for ABP at much higher prices. But now the danger was that too many people would become aware of my plans.

My major sources of capital are a half dozen clients who are familiar with my type of operation. They have made substantial money with me, on balance. True, I have had an occasional lemon, but I always made sure it wasn't too sour. The losses were consistently small and the gains always 100% or more. With the mistakes rarely showing losses of more than 15%, I needed to have only one winner out of six to break even. My ratio of past successes to failures was considerably more favorable.

Most of the capital I needed for the campaign was now lined up, but I wanted an extra edge that would prove useful when I was ready to sell the shares to other buyers at much higher prices. I also sought an escape hatch if market conditions at the time to sell made it difficult to unload the stock.

My trump card was to be Roscoe Lupine, one of the most successful Wall Street "raiders." His particular passion was finding companies whose stock was selling well below liquidation value and where the business was sound but, because of indifferent, incompetent, or dishonest management (often relatives of founding families), the earnings record was poor. Basically, these were situations in which a large amount of capital was immobilized in a company and management was realizing a meager return on it. Lupine would begin buying into the situation until he became a sufficiently large stockholder either to force a change in management, a liquidation of the company (resulting in cash distributions to shareholders far above the market price of the stock), or to bring about mergers on favorable terms.

After I had given him a brief outline of the ABP situation —basically a sound operation, large assets, and now disposing of its losing Magic operation—Lupine was interested. He also wanted to hedge his bets and sought an out if my campaign to run the stock were to prove unsuccessful. After all, he argued, ABP was a dull issue and had dissipated its following. Suppose, at a later date when ABP was prospering again, it proved too difficult again to develop in the public a strong appetite for the stock. One could be left with a piece of paper that would always sell at a large discount from assets and be cheap on earnings.

In response to this, I briefed Lupine on the background of the Magic acquisition, including how Founder III had profited from the merger through the appreciation of the Magic shares bought earlier. In fact, ABP was a suitable candidate for merger into a larger company and on terms that would more accurately reflect its high asset values. But Founder III would doubtless join the unemployed in such event and would oppose a merger. However, fear that the shadier personal aspects of the Magic acquisition would be revealed would certainly make Founder III more responsive to persuasion.

Lupine also had a taste for alchemy. His philosophy was that stocks sell low on the here and now, on the tangible or the probable; they sell high on the possible and highest on the not-impossible. There was food for fantasy in ABP. The value of timber holdings was a major unknown. The sale of the Michigan properties, only a fraction of ABP's total acreage (almost all of which, of course, was not lakeside property), could be used to create an impression that the timber holdings alone were worth hundreds of millions. The chemical research subsidiary could also eventually provide the "not-impossible." I got the commitment from Lupine, for capital now and for cooperation later on. All decisions on tactics and strategy were to be made by me.

Now I was ready to begin my accumulation campaign. Accumulation is a popular, and frequently misapplied, term in the Wall Street lexicon. It means simply bringing together, concentrating ownership of stock in fewer hands. The genesis of the term dates back to the pre-1930 era, when groups controlling substantial capital (called pools) would work in concert to accumulate large positions in specific stocks. The ultimate objective was to create demand for them at higher prices, at which point the accumulators would "distribute" their holdings. Often the distributees were the same persons who had earlier sold the stock to the accumulators at lower prices. The cycle would be complete when the distributees later became disenchanted and sold their stock—at depressed prices —perhaps to accumulators who planned on repeating the cycle.

This accumulation-distribution cycle would usually coincide with the business cycle. When business was good, the public would enter the market and buy stocks, which were obligingly sold to them by those who had had the foresight to anticipate a recovery when times were bad, and to accumulate stocks during the slump.

These groups, or pools, were often identified with insiders such as members of management, who were in the best position to obtain reliable and timely information about the affairs of a company. In addition, they could maneuver the presentation of developments in a manner that would stimulate selling (when they were accumulating) or buying (when they were distributing).

It is difficult in contemporary markets to identify who is assuming which role in this cycle. The small investor has himself increasingly exited from the market, and instead uses intermediaries, either voluntarily chosen ones such as mutual funds, or mandated ones such as penson funds, as a conduit for investment. These intermediaries move huge amounts of money. Since the 1960s they have accumulated (*sic*) huge amounts of stock that have been distributed (*sic*) by relatively small individual stockholders. (In effect, the shareholder as individual has been selling to himself as institution.) So far, judging from the almost total lack of overall market appreciation in the period, the small money (the public) has been far smarter than the big money (the institutions).

Wall Street still tends to characterize any large buying as accumulation, or any buying that comes from reputedly informed sources. This is part of the myth that the wisdom with which money is employed is in direct proportion to its amount and the remoteness of its source. Smart Money is thus either large or alien or both. In this hierarchy, in descending order, Swiss money is genius, Big Money is uniformly intelligent, and Small Money is moronic.

Of course, the probabilities favor Big Money being Smart Money. After all, Big Money has the wherewithal and usually the willingness to buy the best analytical talents. Big Money, who has cocktails with other Big Monies, is often in a position to know firsthand what is going on in a particular business or industry. Today, however, with the divorcement of capital from management, the professional business manager is often better informed than the absentee owner. And he is more likely to be an avid player of the stock market and among the more successful ones. While these executives may not operate in concert with each other, most are privy to the same superior information and thus are most likely to act in the same manner. And, of course, there is a certain ineluctable logic in the proposition that Big Money wouldn't still be Big unless it was also Smart.

It may be less common to see in contemporary markets a concerted agreement among a limited number of people to amass a position in a certain stock, the objective being resale to the public at a later date when certain anticipated good things happen or are believed about to happen. But there is what could be called an accumulative consensus—an agreement of views among informed persons not necessarily in communication with each other that, despite overtly bad news, a stock is a good buy.

The accumulation and distribution concepts serve as handy gimmicks for Wall Street salesmen dealing with clients. The customer never buys more of XYZ as it drops and drops; he "accumulates" it. Through this little magic labeling device, the small brokerage-house client is allowed to equate himself with the sophisticated Big Money player.

As I was now ready to begin buying ABP stock, my first step was to see if there were any big blocks of stock around. If I could start off my campaign with a nucleus of, say, 50,000 shares, I would be well on the way toward my goal. Moreover, I would have enough shares in inventory to exercise a high degree of control over the market action of the stock. My opening volley would be a search for a block of ABP.

8 Testing the Market

When you've been in this business for any length of time, you get to know a lot of institutional salesmen. They are comparable to the customers' man or registered rep or account executive who takes your order to buy 50 shares of American Telephone, but they deal only with large buyers and sellers of stocks, such as mutual funds, the pension funds of companies like U.S. Steel and General Motors, the huge endowment funds of universities, etc. They are accustomed to dealing in blocks of stock running into the hundreds of thousands of shares, worth many millions. One of their special talents is locating parties interested in buying or selling a large block of a specific issue.

As I had frequently acted as a broker for institutional clients, it was easy for me to let it be known that I now had a client (it is always better strategy to pose as intermediary rather than principal) who might be interested in a large block of ABP shares, provided it became available at a worthwhile concession from the current market level—in other words, cheaper than the going price.

Having put out my feelers in the institutional crowd, my next move was to test the market. I wanted some indication of the supply-demand picture: whether I was dealing with a thin market, where sales or purchases of just a few hundred shares would cause wide price swings; whether there was anyone else in the picture as a major buyer; whether it was possible to smoke out some large sellers. When you've been in this business for a while, you have to rely a lot on intuition about market conditions, but it is always desirable to have hard evidence on which to base your diagnosis.

My hunch was that the market situation in ABP was one of potentially plenty of stock for sale and no substantial buying interest. The potential sellers had sat through a two-thirds decline in the value of the shares. Now that the stock had apparently found a resting place in the mid-20s, the owners who had held on this long felt no immediate urgency to sell. There might be some big holders looking for an opportunity to unload, but they wouldn't jettison their stock unless it looked probable that the market could absorb the supply without collapsing, or unless they became frightened that another sharp decline was beginning.

A word on how the auction that is the stock market works. Suppose you want to buy 500 shares of American Telephone. You can ask your broker to get you a "market and size." He might come back with "55 to ¼, 3 by 6." This means that, at that moment, someone is willing to buy 300 shares of American Telephone at 55 while someone else is willing to sell 600 shares at 55¼. That is "the market" in Telephone at that particular moment. If you are in a hurry to get your shares, thinking a rise is imminent, you might tell him to buy the 600 shares offered for sale at 55¼. Unless someone beats you to it, you would then get the shares at that price. Or you might put in your bid for 600 shares at 55⅛ which, of course, would change the market to "55⅛ to ¼, 6 [your 600] by 6." Then, if someone came in to sell shares "at the market" you would get them at 55⅛, since you would be the top bidder.

In such popular stocks as Telephone, General Motors, and U.S. Steel the market is normally broad. By definition, a broad market is one in which the number of shares (size) on both the bid side and the offering side are continuously large, sometimes in multiples of 10,000 shares. And the spread, the difference between the bid price and the asked price, is narrow, perhaps only ⅛ or ¼ of a point. This is one reason why many professional traders deal in only the most active stocks. They know they can buy thousands of shares without forcing prices up, or sell without knocking them down.

ABP was a different matter entirely. A few months ago, when the stock was trading in the 60s and was the Circe of the scalpers, it was not unusual to see thousands of shares of it trade within a ½-point range. Now this leper of the boardrooms would usually be quoted with a ½-point or ¾-point spread, and the size would be 100 to 200 by a similar amount.

My initial purchase was 200 shares at 22½, the quote having been 22⅛ to ½, 1 by 2. The next offering of stock was 100 shares at 22¾. I decided to take the 100 at 22¾ to see what the offerings were at 23. To my surprise the quote became 22½, which represented a token bid by the specialist, to 23, 100 by 900.

A recurrent phenomenon in the stock market is round-number psychology, something professionals often capitalize on. Many people just happen to dislike fractions and prefer round numbers; thus the larger offering at 23. If you happen to be in a boardroom when a popular stock reaches a price of $50 or $100 a share, you will often see large offerings at these figures. That means that members of the public had long ago set their objectives for a multiple of 10 and had entered their sell orders accordingly.

I decided not to take the stock offered at 23 at the moment. The 900 share size was moderately tempting—I had had to move ABP up from 22⅛ to 22¾ just to get 300 shares, and now there were 900 shares that could be gotten for only ¼ point more. But this was an opportunity to see if I had any competing buyers. If others were interested in the situation, they were doubtless sizing up the market and might jump for the 23 block. If so, I might have to readjust my strategy.

But no other buyer appeared, which was the first clue that at that juncture I had no competition for ABP shares. I put in a bid for 200 shares at 22⅝, topping the bidder at 22½ so that in case a few shares came in to be sold "at the market" I would get them. Only 100 shares were offered for sale "at the market" later on that session, and I bought them.

Right after the opening of the market the next day, I "sized" ABP again. I was still top bidder at 22⅝ for 100 (half the order having been already filled the day before), but there were now 200 shares offered for sale at 22¾. Someone had apparently noted the 22⅝ closing the previous day and had decided if he could get ⅛ more, he would be happy. I bought the 200 shares at 22¾ and now the quote became 22½–23, but by now the offering had increased to 1,800 shares. Perhaps the round number that had looked unattainable just a few sessions back was now proving a magnet for more owners waiting to dispose of their positions.

I decided to take some of the offering but not all of it. I waited until minutes before the close of the market and then bought 1,400 of the shares at 23. Within four minutes three additional trades of 100 shares each followed. Aha! Circe had not lost her lure for some. The sudden activity in ABP—a 500-share block had become a rarity in recent weeks—had not escaped the voyeurs in the boardrooms, and perhaps conjured up visions of the 3- or 5-point jumps that had characterized ABP's performance just a few months back. Something must be cooking, thought they, and decided to jump on the bandwagon.

By taking only part of the stock offered at 23, I had ensured there would be enough still available at that price to satisfy the few scalpers who might decide to chase it. If the advance by ABP shares appeared to be "meeting stock" (*i.e.*, plentiful offerings) at 23, it would scare off any other venturesome traders and prevent a sustainable rally from developing. My strategy worked; no additional buyers entered the picture. At two minutes before the market's close, I put in an order to sell 300 shares "at the market," and 100 were sold at 22½, 100 at 22¼, and 100 at 22⅛.

The casual examiner of the stock price tables in the newspaper the next day saw that ABP closed at 22⅛, off ½ point for the session on unusually high volume, compared with recent sessions, of about 2,000 shares. This was more than double the average daily turnover in the stock for the past few weeks. Was this a sign that some substantial unloading was underway? Perhaps ABP, which had been battered by waves of liquidation all the way down from the 60s, was in for another siege by sellers.

By now, you have gotten an insight into my strategy. A rather obvious but profound truth is that traders and investors buy stocks because they think the stocks will go up in price. For traders, the most convincing evidence that stocks are going up is that they are going up. Conversely, traders avoid stocks that are declining, and the most convincing evidence that they will decline in price is that they are declining in price. Wall Street is unique in the annals of merchandising. Only there does one mark *up* merchandise in order to make it more attractive and move it out of inventory more rapidly.

The stock ticker, whether Trans-Lux, paper tape, or modern electronic display, is the most potent point-of-purchase (or point-of-sale) advertising medium in the world. The message of my merchandising campaign was that "ABP is a loser, sell it," and the action of the stock was screaming to the tape watchers, "Sell me, I am going down." Keep in mind that there is no extrapolator like the inveterate trader who always follows trends rather than anticipates changes in them.

Some customers were obviously convinced by my late-day selling of the 300 shares "at market." The next morning, ABP opened at 400 shares at 22, evidently sold by holders who had become nervous at the preceding day's performance. Some more stock came onto the market, and I took shares at 21 and a fraction. This slow decline in the stock price was to be the pattern for some weeks to come. Occasionally, when someone would offer a larger piece of perhaps 700 or 1,000 shares above the existing market, I would take the stock up to get the block, knocking it down again at the close of the day, if necessary, by selling a few hundred shares. As long as no one else was interested in taking a sizable position in ABP, I need fear only the competition from the short-term traders. I made sure they were burned frequently enough that they wouldn't be active buyers.

This strategy produced a corollary advantage. The "action" of the stock's price was so poor that it attracted short sellers —not a large number, but a few thousand shares over a period of weeks. They, of course, were selling stock they didn't yet own, intending to buy later on the open market at lower prices. They would then deliver the shares, closing out their positions at a profit—or so they planned. Instead, much later, by a stroke of Wall Street fate, they were to be my unwitting helpers in accelerating the rise in the price of the stock.

During the time that I was buying a few hundred shares of ABP daily on the open market, the feelers to institutional salesmen had evoked some response. It was now toward the end of the year, when many mutual funds undertake what is called window dressing, or year-end housecleaning. The custom is to realign portfolios so that at the close of the reporting period (quarterly and at the end of the year) some of the mistakes will not be so glaringly obvious to fund shareholders. As the dates and prices of sales during the period are not specified in the report, it is left to the shareholders to guess how shrewd or foolish the portfolio manager has been.

At the time of the secondary offering by the two founders of Magic, who had sold their 400,000 shares of ABP stock at 65, two large blocks—one of 50,000 shares and the other of 100,000 shares—had been placed with two separate mutual funds. From the market action of the stock during the decline, it was possible that one of those blocks had been sold. However, I felt at least one block was probably still intact, held by a mutual fund.

ABP had fluctuated between a high of 42 and a low of 21 in the last two months and was now within a fraction of the low. If the shares were still in a fund's portfolio at year-end, and ABP were selling at 21, the 44-point paper loss from the 65 purchase price would be an embarrassment indeed to the fund management; it could not escape notice by shareholders. If the block of ABP were sold during the final quarter, the sales price would not be revealed and shareholders could easily surmise that the fund had gotten close to the top price (42) during that period for their stock. It would still be a loss, yes, but only half of what a year-end market quote of 21 would represent.

It turned out that the Conservative Management Fund still had the 100,000-share block of ABP that it had bought on the secondary at 65. My informant, one of the more aggressive institutional salesmen who, incidentally, had originally gotten Conservative interested in ABP, told me that Conservative "might be willing" to consider selling their stock but they felt the market was seriously undervaluing ABP. They were thinking more in terms of $30 a share but "could be flexible." To me this meant they wanted out but didn't want to take such a huge licking.

This 100,000-share block could prove the key to my whole campaign; I wanted those shares and I wanted them badly. But I didn't want them at 30. If I could get the block, it would save me months of laborious accumulation on the open market, during which period there was always the risk of having the market get away from me. Someone else might become interested in the situation. Competition from another substantial buyer could force me to bid up for the stock, significantly reducing my potential profit.

I knew I wasn't going to be dealing with a babe in the woods. Conservative had made a blunder in buying ABP—and a big one—but it was a fund noted for its sophistication in trading and its insight into the mechanics of the market. However, I knew they had a strong incentive to sell by year-end, while they had no clue as to how anxious I was to get their block. A meeting was quickly arranged between Derek Wasppe, manager of the Conservative Investment Committee, and myself for the following week.

9 Gamesmanship

Leaving my office to go to my initial lunch meeting with Wasppe, I reviewed the progress of my campaign in ABP. My position now amounted to close to 17,000 shares, bought at an average price of $22 a share. As the end of the year approached, sellers of the stock were entering the market in greater force. I could buy about 800 shares of ABP a day without noticeably affecting the price level, but at this rate it could be several months before a substantial position could be accumulated.

Time, for the next few weeks, was on my side. It was now the middle of November, the tax-loss selling season. This is the period of the Great Catharsis: Take your losses, runs the assuaging rationalization, not because you made a mistake, but so that you can utilize the loss in order to offset gains for tax purposes. Never mind that you may not have any gains to begin with. This is the perfect occasion to play the affluent masochist, savoring his losses.

There was still no real competition for ABP shares, although the tax-loss seller has his counterpart in the year-end bargain hunter. This breed shops around for "down from the high" issues in late December, figuring that he can scalp 2 or 3 points by selling in the first weeks in January, when the pressure from tax selling abates and, like an extended rubber band, prices rebound.

My first encounter with Wasppe offered no surprises. Somehow, I knew that I wasn't going to like this man, and I didn't. I started out with the premise that he was stupid—how else could he have gotten into ABP in the mid-60s in the first place? I was angry at him for dissipating the assets of naïve fundholders. And, to be honest, I was envious that this boob could have investment control over so many scores of millions of dollars although he had probably never made a decent capital gain in his life with his own money. Ah, what pools could be organized with the kind of capital his fund could swing!

Our meeting was formal and cool. After the usual pleasantries, the overture consisted of some chitchat about the market. Wasppe was remarkable in his ability to say nothing that would embarrass him later on, while appearing positive and decisive. If you asked him if he thought the market would go higher or lower, he would declaim that "unquestionably there are going to be some violent swings." On the other hand, if you proposed some definitive proposition—such as that the economy was going to boom vigorously for the next few years, or a recession was imminent—he would reply quite earnestly that he "wouldn't be a bit surprised if the forecasters of doom [or boom] were surprised." And of course, when asked to take a position on any economic and market question, he would feign diffidence and, while parroting what the crowd was saying, protest that his was "a minority view."

When we finally got down to the issue at hand, a possible transfer of the large block of ABP stock, Wasppe launched into what was for him a spirited disquisition on the inefficiency of the marketplace in reflecting value. His conclusion was that "ABP is depressed well below its real value. It is only because our security analysts have discovered other, more suitable investment vehicles that we would consider selling out our position anywhere near the current market." Can it be that the fund had found an even greater bargain than it had perceived ABP to be?

I was in no mood to argue over the validity of the market as a "mirror of value." Wasppe had spoken his piece, and my almost obtuse, vague rejoinder signaled that I considered his remarks irrelevant. He had given no overt clue as to how anxious he was to bury this albatross before the close of the year. And I was equally determined to give no hint of how eager I was to buy his block of stock. We parted with the understanding that, having established an identity, if not a rapport, for each other, we would have further discussions at an undetermined later date.

I still felt strongly that, in dealing with Wasppe, time was on my side. December 31 meant much to him but held no magic for me. I would wait for him to make the next overture.

November passed and I still hadn't heard from Wasppe. It was now the first week in December. Perhaps I had overestimated his eagerness to sell? But my anxiety was unwarranted. On Wednesday, December 10, Wasppe called, suggesting we have lunch again and "chat about the ABP situation." I indicated that I would, of course, be happy to meet with him again and suggested we make our appointment for about two weeks later, on the twenty-third. My strategy was to enter into any negotiations for the purchase of shares as close to the thirty-first as possible, when pressure to sell would be mounting.

Wasppe replied that he would be out of town during the end of December (quick thinking, I decided) and suggested later this week or early the following week. Unfortunately, I explained, my calendar was pretty full (my only firm engagement during the next two weeks was with my barber), but I could make it on Wednesday the seventeenth at the Puritan Club.

During the first week of December I was able to pick up a

bit more stock: close to 1,500 shares a day, priced around 21. Suddenly, on Friday the twelfth, just three trading sessions before my scheduled meeting with Wasppe, ABP became a little more actively traded and began to advance. Almost 3,000 shares changed hands on Friday—I bought none of them—and the stock advanced to 22½. On random occasions before, some small buyer had taken the market away from me for a few hours and I had always stepped away, sure that once the bidder had obtained a few hundred shares he would decamp and let the stock fall again into my waiting basket.

On this occasion, however, it was not just a small buyer in the picture. It was obvious that it was just one buyer and that he wanted his stock *now*. I kept quoting the market—the sizes of the bids and offerings—and noted that the buyer never waited for the seller to lose patience and sell to him at the market. Instead, this buyer took each offering on the way up as soon as it was put on the books. By the end of the day, he had probably bought 2,500 shares of ABP.

It is premature to jump to conclusions from just one day's action. Since it is a composite of the actions of millions of individuals, the market abounds in random price moves that have no particular significance. The timing of an investment decision or even the choice of a particular stock frequently has to do only with matters relating to the buyer, not to externals. The stock was not "well bought"; the buyer had only to top other bids to get all the stock he wanted, he didn't have to chase it. If he could have waited, the stock would come to him. Moreover, by causing the stock price to rise rapidly, the buyer would actually discourage potential sellers: After all, some Joe Triste would think, as he was about to part with the 100 shares he'd bought at higher levels a few months ago, ABP "is acting so well" that there must be something afoot! This stock is going up—the best reason on earth not to sell it.

Perhaps, I thought suddenly, this buyer had some good reason to be in a hurry. Perhaps he was privy to promising developments not generally known. But a call to Confrer re-assured me that nothing new had happened to ABP. The negotiations for the sale of Magic were proceeding smoothly, but no deal had yet been signed. The company was planning no surprising goodies for the financial community.

Having received that confirmation from Confrer, I was again unnerved when ABP opened on Monday a point above the closing Friday price! The first sale was 500 at 24, fol-lowed by a few 100- and 200-share lots that brought it up to 25. I was concerned because ABP had become a "thin stock" —there were normally no large orders to sell or to buy, and a small momentary imbalance in the supply-demand equation could translate into disproportionately large price moves.

Then through an associate on the Stock Exchange floor I found out that the buying was, in fact, coming from one house: Brown, Grant and Grey, an old-line firm known for serving institutional clients. The picture was becoming clear. Of course the buyer didn't want to amass a position at the lowest cost—the buyer was interested only in having ABP shares move higher. It had to be Wasppe.

And Wasppe had succeeded. By buying perhaps 5,000 shares at an average price of 22 or so, Wasppe had been able to increase the market value of the fund's 100,000 shares from 21 to 25 (or by $400,000) with an outlay of $100,000. From another perspective, this $100,000 expenditure had in-creased the total market value of ABP's 2.1 million outstand-ing shares by $8.4 million. Fantastic? No, it happens every day. "Values" in the stock market depend on that little incre-ment, that extra margin of buying or selling, demand or supply, that determines current prices.

It was now obvious to me that Wasppe was setting the table for our luncheon, and planning to serve me crow. And he had a good chance of selecting the menu unless I got into the kitchen, fast. Already, some of the denizens of the board-rooms were noting the "good action." To them, a rise in the price of a stock is enough to constitute good action. Perhaps Wasppe could start a run on the stock! It was thin, a few dozen shrewd scalpers could start fireworks, perhaps attract the professional floor traders—and my campaign to accumulate a large position at bargain levels would, at least temporarily, be stymied.

Wasppe's campaign had succeeded in attracting some interest but not yet enough. My strategy was to counter sloppy buying with sloppy selling. It was now eleven-thirty on Monday, two days before our scheduled lunch meeting, and ABP was holding at 25, where, for the moment, small sellers and small buyers were evenly matched. Again, I took into consideration that boardrooms would be crowded during the lunch hour. This could prove an expensive advertising campaign for Wasppe. He had already spent perhaps a hundred grand to popularize the slogan "Buy Me, I'm Going Up." I would risk selling a few thousand shares from my position to create dissatisfied customers, evoking a counterslogan: "Sell Me, I'm Still a Dog."

At eleven-thirty I entered an order to sell 700 shares at the market, which was then 25 bid and 25½ offered, 2 by 2. My offering was a fairly sizable piece for ABP under the existing circumstances. I wanted Wasppe's broker on the floor to get the impression, for the moment, that this was the complete holding of the seller. If I had thrown in a few thousand shares to sell at the market, the broker might have dropped his bid a point or so, taken my offering at the depressed price, and then bid aggressively for a few hundred shares, in order to run up the price again. But 700 shares looked like a random piece, perhaps cleaning out that particular seller. The ploy apparently worked. Wasppe's broker took the shares at 25. The quote was still 25–25¼.

It was now about noon and the critical moment had arrived. I immediately put in an order to sell 4,000 shares down to 24. This meant that my broker was to continue selling shares until

the price fell to 24. He was to fill all bids until the market became 23¾ and bid my offer at 24. My objective was to knock
the stock down to 24 and then put a cap on it. Wasppe's broker
would see that the sell order came from the same broker who
had offered the 700 shares moments before. I hoped he would
wonder how large a seller was standing in the wings, how
much stock would he have to "eat" to hold up the price. To
take 4,000 shares at one clip without any guarantee that there
might not be another 4,000, perhaps 10,000, still to be sold
was too big a risk. As I had hoped, Wasppe's broker immediately stepped away. A hundred shares were sold at 25, 200 at
24½, and 500 at 24. Now the market was 23½–24, 1 by
3,200—the remaining balance of my 4,000 share sell order.

In effect, I had put a ceiling on the stock. Unless Wasppe
was willing to take the risk that he was not seeing the tip of an
iceberg, he would back away from his mark-up campaign
and be forced to let the market find its own level. My advertising campaign had its impact on the boardrooms. Now, ABP
was "acting poorly," said the sedentary sages, and there were
no traders willing to grab a few shares in hopes of a turn
upward.

The scalpers who had bought earlier in the session and who
had jumped in on the preceding Friday were now willing to
take their 2-point licking and get out. ABP eased back to 22½,
closing off 1½ points for the day. Tuesday was largely more
of the same. The stock opened on a few hundred shares at 22
—I had stepped away completely as buyer or seller—and had
drifted down to 21 by late afternoon. In the last hour of trading I sold 500 shares at the market, knocking ABP down to
20¼, just ⅛ above its low. Now, it was my turn to set the
table.

The next day was Wednesday, and my luncheon appointment with Wasppe was at one-thirty. ABP opened on a 700-
share piece at 20, a new low. The previous day's action had

triggered decisions by some nervous holders who had previously been stupefied by disgust, and now were motivated to act by revived fear. The new low invited more selling, and ABP had receded to fractionally above 18 as I prepared to go to the Puritan Club, a Victorian combination of high ceilings, marble floors, unadorned wood paneling, antiseptic victuals, septuagenarian waiters, and an old-fashioned ticker-tape machine handily located in the cloakroom. Timing was of the essence in my plan. Wasppe, I had learned from our previous meeting, was a two-cocktail, three-course, two-cigar luncher. The afternoon meal was designed more to pad the day than to take nourishment. It was unlikely we would be getting down to brass tacks before two-fifteen at the earliest.

I instructed my office to sell a few hundred shares of ABP at the market around 1 P.M., then to step up the liquidation at 2 P.M., continuing to sell until ABP receded below 18. Stock was to be continuously offered for sale to prevent ABP from rising above 18 before two-thirty.

Wasppe was prompt and, as we got down to lunch, I informed him that I had to leave promptly at two-thirty to catch a plane to Boston. This was an outright lie, but the message was unambiguous that our transaction was not of paramount importance to me, nor of pressing urgency. While I quickly demolished a crabmeat cocktail and enjoyed a large, rare steak, Wasppe rambled on about the economy and the stock market, and over his third martini indicted market inefficiency, as evidenced by the undervaluation of ABP shares.

Finally, over Indian pudding, Wasppe got down to price. He was willing to split the difference between yesterday's closing price, 20, and what he had been originally asking, 30 a share. "It's a giveaway at 25, but the fund has other fish to fry" was how he explained this compromise. I replied that he was way out of line and that my client now demanded a concession from the market and was not willing to pay over 17 for the stock. Whether Wasppe knew I was just using a

negotiating ploy was problematical, but he expressed surprise at the unreasonably low figure. Indeed, his surprise was
so great that he spilled a little coffee on his trousers and immediately excused himself to go to the men's room. I noted
that it was now exactly two-twenty.

Moments later, Wasppe returned, smiling and casual.
Where were we? Between 25 and 17, I replied.

"The devil. Let's make it 20, and the 100,000 shares are
sold." He laughed magnanimously. I admired his style, but
I am no philanthropist. "My client insists on a concession
from market. Let's split the difference and make it 18½. Now
I've got to get out of here and catch a plane." I got up. The
movement smacked of "take it or leave it." Wasppe stood up,
put his hand out, and said, "Agreed." We shook hands and the
deal was set. We both smiled—whose relief was the greater
I do not know—and then we walked to the checkroom to get
our coats. We passed, without turning, the Stock Exchange
ticker, rattling out the stuff of dreams. "By the way, are you
in the market for any more stock?" asked Wasppe. "Perhaps
a bit more," I replied. "I think I know where 15,000 additional shares are. Do you want them? At the same price?"
"I'll take them," I said, and again we shook hands.

While I put on my coat, Wasppe went over to the ticker,
lifted the freshly printed prices coming out on the narrow
ribbon, and remarked with apparent surprise, "Oops, I see
ABP has broken 17." I ambled over, saw ABP go by at 16⅞.
The clock stood at two-thirty. "Well sold, Wasppe," I smiled,
with obvious philosophic resignation.

PART II

10   Layers of

Reality

To those unfamiliar with its workings, Wall Street has usually been viewed as the Superman of institutions, eminently rational and pragmatic, with more than a touch of prescience. The well-known and generally misunderstood Dow Theory is premised on the existence of a large body of knowledgeable "insiders" (known in common parlance as "they") who buy and sell at just the right time by virtue of their superior insight into, and knowledge of, the economy. Our society as a matter of course rewards their knowledgeability with formidable wealth, so they always have the means to implement their judgment.

The performance of the stock market in recent years should have left the exalted reputation of the "they's" sullied indeed. The sagacity that impels the "they's" to buy at the bottom just before business turns up and then sell to the "you's" at the peak just before everything turns sour has proved somewhat imperfect. The panic decline of the spring of 1962—reflecting as much liquidation by professional portfolio managers as by the Unwashed You's—occurred just as the economy was embarking upon a record-breaking period of vigorous expansion and prosperity.

Again in the spring of 1965—apparently the fancy frequently turns to cash rather than common stocks in this season —average stock prices tumbled in response to the sophisticates' anxiety about an impending devaluation of the British pound and a run on the dollar. As prices fell, the myth of the market's prescience came into play and the economists chorused that doom was imminent.

Incidentally, this was a period when the professionals had the market largely to themselves. The small investor (or speculator, depending on whether you care to editorialize) had stood by passively for years while the professionals had gobbled up the bargains and later disgorged them in a frenzy of sudden pessimism. The small investor had imprudently demurred to the superior wisdom of the professionals by selling the stock he owned, and with the proceeds, sadly, purchased professional advice packaged as mutual funds.

Whatever remnants of respectability that professional portfolio management, as exemplified by the large institutions, still commanded should have been irretrievably compromised in 1974. The autumn of that year saw the Great Institutional Panic that brought stock prices to the lowest level in over a decade in a frenzy of disgorgement by insurance companies and other "sophisticated" professionals. And who came out of the sticks to snatch up what subsequently proved historical bargains? The Middle American individual investor who, paying for his stocks with cash, suddenly became a net buyer.

The experience of the past few years suggests that whatever remote connection there ever was between business and the stock market has become even more tenuous. Perhaps one important reason is that there is a less than rational correlation between the stock of a company and the company itself, *i.e.*, its plants, personnel, products, profits, *et cetera.* In a consumer economy, the consumer is king, we are led to understand. If his choice is the appearance of things, rather than the thing itself, or the peripheral rewards in the form of status, security, respectability, or what have you, then the marketplace adjusts to his wants. And the stock market has done so admirably, perhaps at considerable penalty to the efficiency of its capital-allocating function.

While a stock certificate represents a share in the ownership of the assets of a particular business, it has also become a piece of paper that has an autonomous personality of its own. Market performance of the shares themselves is often the most important determinant in the attitude of prospective buyers and sellers toward this piece of paper. Carrying this approach to its ultimate absurdity, the most sophisticated traders on Wall Street are completely uninterested in what company or business is represented by the piece of paper with the symbol XYZ on the ticker tape. The stock XYZ—the piece of paper— either acts well or acts poorly, and this attracts either buying or selling. This same action/reaction is true of the stock market as a whole and goes a long way toward explaining the self-perpetuating momentum of trends.

I have sometimes wondered whether some of the names that habitually occur on the most active trading lists were not fictitious. Perhaps Wall Streeters, particularly the commission-oriented retail brokerage houses, have just invented the symbol to be traded back and forth in huge volume, generating handsome revenues in the form of commissions, while no real operating business actually exists. I am reminded of the old story about the traders who were extremely active in the canned sardine market. Turnover was enormous and prices advanced dramatically. One day a trader found himself in possession of an actual can of the sardines. Upon opening the can, he found the contents were rotten. When he complained to another trader, he was quickly told: "You are not supposed to *open* the can. These are *trading* sardines, not *eating* sardines."

There are still many substantial investors who consider this purely "technical" approach to stock selection slightly immoral and smacking of charlatanism. They insist that there be something "fundamentally" attractive about a company's situation. Too often, the fundamental appeal they find is based on a carefully orchestrated effort to create among investors an image that bears only a casual relationship to the business realities. In this type of public relations campaign, if one wants to sell a stock at the most remote relationship to traditional ideas of value, it is important that there be a "concept."

As a result of this divorcement between the stock and the company, there has developed on Wall Street an industry devoted to creating images for stocks. Its function is to create customers for the shares themselves, not for the products or services offered by the company that the stock represents. The techniques involved are complex and nebulous, but once an image is created, it becomes largely self-sustaining. Assuming there ever was a relationship to the underlying reality of the company, the connection may disappear through changes in the company's operations, but the image will remain.

The miracle of successful image creation is that ownership of a stock may evoke such psychic rewards (since the rewards are frequently only nominal in terms of dividends) that all holders will be happy, and therefore unwilling to part with their prized possession, while nonowners will want desperately to join the inner circle and share the psychic rewards. And they will happily pay dear prices relative to a stock's tangible earnings and dividends for the privilege.

A successful "image stock" brings an aura of enchantment, visions of infinite capital gains—always on paper, but never to be realized through actual sale of one's holdings. Moreover, the image helps the company itself fulfill such sanguine expectations. If a company's stock sells high in relation to earnings, it can trade expensive image paper for nonimage companies. The image prevails, and the earnings of the combined companies enjoy the high price-earnings ratio of the image company—a surefire formula for capital enhancement.

Creating an image for ABP products was my next, and a difficult, task. The business was prosaic and, even worse, there were many other concerns also engaged in converting forest products into building materials. There were, however, a few factors common to the industry and some unique to ABP that could be exploited for image-creating purposes.

Population explosion was a convenient concept to glamorize the gradual secular growth in home demand. ABP could be singled out as unique in a pedestrian industry through its "aggressiveness" (an extremely popular but singularly meaningless word on Wall Street), leadership, and imagination. Although the Magic venture had doubtless left a soiled picture of ABP in the minds of the glamour-oriented stock buyers, the chemical research company could prove the alluring "kicker," that unquantifiable bonus that suggests the possibility of open-ended gains. For the inflationphobe, hundreds of thousands of acres of owned timberland were the lure.

An important function of the image would be to dissuade present shareholders from quickly selling their stock in the event of any rise. After all, I didn't want to have to buy the whole capitalization in order to advance the price. And the more optimistic the shareholders, the easier it would be to move the price higher; there would be less stock to absorb on the way up.

The shareholders could be influenced only by better communication from the company. In the past, Founder III himself had written the president's message in the annual report, the pronouncements appearing in quarterly statements, and releases to the newspapers. He had also established a procedure under which all inquiries from Wall Street brokerage houses or from the press were referred directly to him. He had assumed preemptive control of communications ever since it had appeared that the Magic acquisition was becoming a catastrophe.

The time had certainly arrived for a comprehensive program that would develop an attitude among shareholders, existing and prospective, that would be propitious for my campaign, the objective of which was to eventually create an active, exuberant, and substantially higher market for ABP shares. My expertise in orchestrating the performance of the stock would be the ultimate key to success; the immediate task was to assume control over the internal workings of the company.

Confrer was ideally suited for this role. He alone among the members of the board had created no enemies, offered no recriminations, and had had no active hand in the mistakes of the past. A chastened chief executive and a lethargic board were now quite willing, even anxious, to be directed by Confrer. So he would act as my agent in steering management along the course I believed best suited to my objective.

The annual report for the year in which the Magic fiasco had occurred was a scanty four-page affair, containing only the minimum information required by the SEC dotted with incomprehensible accounting footnotes. The president's message had been vague and uninformative, offering no insight into what had happened to the company or where it was going. The quarterly reports had been confined to the necessary figures on sales, expenses, and earnings. Thus, shareholders received neither pleasure from the statistics (which showed sharply lower earnings in recent periods), nor solace from excuses or explanations, nor hope from bright projections for the future. This made for an unhappy marriage between shareholder and corporation.

The report for the July-September quarter, already issued,

lacked anything that could inspire hope in the shareholders that better times were coming, and consequently provided no solace for those seeking a justification to cling to a losing proposition. It is amazing how responsive the stockholder who is sitting with a large unrealized "paper" loss that is growing larger every day can be to the slightest bit of official encouragement. He is simply yearning for any dim reason to avoid admitting he has made a mistake.

It was now late January, and the new annual report would not be out for another two months or so. The negotiations for disposing of the Magic subsidiary had not yet produced a binding agreement, so questions remained on accounting treatment, which would be affected by the final terms of the sale of the Magic subsidiary as well as by decisions by the board of directors and the accounting firm. Little tangible hope could be offered ABP's shareholders.

The first decision made was to issue a preliminary statement to shareholders by Founder III, the president. It was to be vague but couched in intimate, informal terms. Reference was made to the difficulties incurred in certain (unspecified) operations, and shareholders were assured that aggressive steps were being taken to overcome them. In addition, the statement mentioned that a reorganization of management and of facilities was being undertaken to improve overall efficiency. This program, combined with intensive cost-reduction measures, gave rise to a "sincere personal conviction" that your company was again "well on the road toward sustained long-term growth."

There was nothing concrete here, to be sure—but perhaps enough for the wavering stockholder to grasp as justification for transforming an unfortunate short-term speculation into a long-term investment.

The next step was designed to raise the morale of the company's employees and management. ABP had over 2,000 employees, each one a potential booster or knocker of the company and its stock. If they became stockholders, they would have a tangible incentive to be more productive workers—or should we say, co-owners—and through their families and friends a nucleus could be created of 10,000 or more persons who had something to gain from a rise in the price of ABP shares.

As a means of achieving this objective, two programs were instituted, one for executives and the other for nonmanagement personnel. Executives were given stock options. The price was based on the market price at the time the program was instituted, but the exercise price was increased by 5% each year. The options were exercisable at $25 through the current year, $26.25 the next, $27.56 the following year, *etc.* The formula gave executives an incentive for early execution of their options and another motive for speeding up operating improvement.

A thrift program was introduced for all other employees, enabling them to buy stock at 70% of the market price, with the company contributing the balance. These programs added a few thousand persons—employees and their families—to those who had an interest in the company's making more money and the stock's selling higher. Although composed of amateurs, it was a public relations force of potentially formidable impact.

Having taken steps to motivate shareholders to retain their stock and to provide employees with an interest in the shares' selling higher, the next move was to inspire sponsorship from Wall Street brokerage houses and build up interest among institutional investors. This is where a more public revamping of the image was to figure.

11 Creating

an Image

Wall Street is a complex institution, enamored of its own myths and values, which must be dealt with on their own terms. While ABP as a company would remain what it had always been—a straightforward, successful factor in a prosaic business—we were aiming for a picture of a dynamic, aggressively managed investment vehicle in an exciting industry.

The new image had two facets, the company and the management. We were aiming at a more liberal appraisal of ABP on the basis of its operations and a bonus premium thrown in for unusually efficient management. This is perhaps counting the same trick twice—the operations of the company reflect the efficiency, or lack thereof, of management—but Wall Street is prone to count the same tricks often, if it is winning.

The campaign to upgrade the standing of management revolved around enhancing the prestige of Founder III as a leader in the industry, and as a forward thinker. His name was little known either on Wall Street or in the industry, which was actually an advantage. No one associated the Magic fiasco with Founder III personally. With an unknown, creating the desired public image was less difficult.

An expensive public relations outfit was retained, one whose name you would never recognize. Its biggest assets were its past successes and its anonymity to the public. It was no problem for them to arrange for Founder III to address the next annual convention of the Residential Contractors Society. A simple but statesmanlike speech was written for him. The basic theme, which was unrelated to ABP, was "Are we building nineteenth-century homes for twentieth-century America?"

The theme was catchy and inoffensive. The question was posed and some interesting information proffered on how many products used in homes today are exactly the same as they were a hundred years ago. The speech did some editorializing but was not critical enough to offend anyone in the construction industry. One teaser in the speech was to provide a source of "magic" later on. Founder III alluded to the ultimate development of revolutionary forestry management techniques and of new products from the forest industry's waste products that would result in substantially lower costs and, of course, higher profits for the industry.

News releases, tailor-made for various newspapers from the *Podunk Weekly Ledger* to the *New York Times*, were prepared and sent throughout the country. Any editor needing a filler was our target. The theme of nineteenth-century homes for twentieth-century Americans was emphasized, but it was entangled with the name of Founder III and, incidentally, ABP. The exposure was broad and favorable.

A few weeks later, the next step was taken. ABP announced that a grant had been made to Yale University for research into "solutions to the problem of the underhoused in America," with particular emphasis on how private capital could be mobilized to ameliorate the situation. Harvard had been considered for the grant, but that institution was considered too controversial.

Coinciding with the grant, Founder III addressed the National Cultural Foundation. This took a little doing, but a handsome contribution paved the way. The speech was again a vague rehash of the problem of inadequate housing in the U.S. and its cultural ramifications. The emphasis, however, was not on the poor but on the millions of affluent Americans who are "housed but homeless." Again the indictment was not of the industry, building contractors, unions, or anyone in particular. The phrase was the thing, and it caught on.

The image-building program was an immediate success. Founder's name was brought before the newspaper-reading public under such circumstances that everyone thought he was already well known to everyone else. The latecomers were quick to add the name of Founder III to those in public life who were "policy makers." He was viewed as an imaginative businessman with a sense of responsibility to the community. Some of the favorable impression naturally rubbed off on ABP.

The next step was to dramatize the image of a more aggressive management. The corporation announced some major changes, the most important of which was the creation of a new Department of Development and Expansion. Named to head the newly created division was a former vice-president of one of the most dynamic companies in the industry. The implications were obvious: ABP was about to embark upon a more active expansion program.

Next, some institutional advertisements were placed in *Fortune* magazine and in the *Wall Street Journal*. A new corporate emblem had been designed and the slogan "Living Room for a Space Age" adopted. The advertisements were ostensibly aimed at attracting contractors who would be customers for ABP building products. Their real objective was to bring the name of the company before thousands of executives and security analysts and investors, potential customers for ABP stock.

The program was beginning to have an effect. Speaking invitations came to Founder III, mostly from small organizations that felt their names would gain prestige from an identification with this increasingly prominent businessman. One invitation was from the International Society of Architects, to round out the image by adding the color of statesmanship. Coincidentally with acceptance of this invitation, Avantius, the famous Italian architect, was named consultant for design and new product development.

The Founder III's subject at this conference was to be "The U.S. as Builder for the World," an appeal this time to enlightened chauvinism. The theme emphasized that Americans were the best-housed people in the world and the American building industry the most efficient, able to compete anywhere in the world. It was proposed that the U.S. should now embark upon a program of exporting its expertise, not as a "giveaway" or charity, but in a businesslike fashion. Huge international markets were envisioned, awaiting the enterprising American concerns that chose to go after them. "Our greatest export is expertise." The speech received a surprisingly good reception, so good, in fact, that ABP two weeks later announced the formation of a new International Division to investigate the potentials in overseas markets.

On the New York Stock Exchange, the stock had done a little better, moving to around 30, but this may have reflected a gradually increasing awareness that the company, now that Magic was being disposed of, could soon begin making decent profits. However, impact of the program on the investment community was more tangible. ABP executive offices now received at least two calls a week from brokerage houses that wanted to send an analyst to interview management. In the entire preceding six months, a total of only three inquiries had been received at the company.

But the moment had not yet arrived for wide dissemination of the story of ABP's turnabout in earnings. First, there was to be some groundwork laid to obtain sponsorship from the appropriate Wall Street houses. It was vitally important that the right people have a position in ABP stock near current levels—so they would have a strong incentive to see it rise substantially. The mark-up phase had just begun, and sponsorship would be vital to its success and to creating a climate conducive to my disposing of a large position at a handsome profit. About $3 million was riding on the success of this campaign; I would leave nothing to chance.

12 Sponsorship

Having laid the groundwork for a better public reception for ABP stock, the next step was to attract sponsorship, the right kind of sponsorship, for the stock. In a world where cause-and-effect relationships are remotely connected at best —and more often completely imaginary—"sponsorship" is often improperly used to characterize the motivating force behind a stock's rise. Most frequently, a stock price will rise simply because of a randomly generated desire to own the stock, with buyers acting out of their own unarticulated and often irrational motives. Price, at least over finite periods of time, is a function of urgency—urgency to own a particular piece of paper, or urgency to exchange it for cash. The boardroom savant, when asked why Egregiously Touted Ltd. is rising, will mutter knowingly, "Sponsorship." *The* causal factor is thus immediately isolated and the questioner is either satisfied with a simple single cause or unwilling to betray his naïveté by asking for an elaboration on the answer "sponsorship."

Not that sponsorship is pure myth. By no means—when it is actually present, it makes stocks rise, often with little regard for their fundamental merit, and the rise, in turn, makes others anxious to share in the ownership. Sponsorship is a dynamic element that influences the acceptance of a particular issue by an investor or speculator. In its simplest form, sponsorship is a recommendation of a particular issue by a brokerage house. If Affluent, Vieux Lucre & Bros. are believed to be bullish on XYZ, and the Bros. have a reputation for backing winners, then XYZ will probably prove to be a winner. Although the parallel may offend the fastidious, it is much like the horse player who consistently bets on a hot jockey.

Any Wall Street house of genuine merit is jealous of its reputation for successful sponsorship. It will not knowingly back a doubtful or meretricious situation. After all, the ability of a house to sponsor successfully is comparable to a goose capable of laying many, many golden eggs, and it weights the probabilities that any venture backed by a house with a good reputation will be a winner. If enough owners and potential stock buyers believe that XYZ will prove a winner, it will probably develop into one. There are always enough intangibles in stock appraisals to justify a higher price for A than for B, even though the more skeptical analyst may not see the fine distinctions. And the successful sponsor has to be careful because ultimately the merits of a company will determine where the stock sells, although admittedly within a wide range. If the sponsor's darlings stretch credibility or prove to be outright lemons, the magic wand quickly loses its power.

Sponsoring houses often specialize in different types of companies. Some confine themselves to growth issues and develop a whole industry concept that will provide justification for paying today for the earnings projected for ten years hence. Another may have an articulate analyst with a facile vocabulary in the physical sciences. Its specialty may be sophisticated technology issues—the sophistication in inverse ratio to the probability of an early marketing of an exotic product. Other sponsoring houses may concentrate on "special situations." Argentte, Mewlaugh and Doe was just such a house, and ABP fitted neatly into this category.

Cash Argentte was widely known—and envied—on Wall

Street. His enemies characterized him as ruthless and avaricious; his friends as unsentimental and pragmatic. He was called successful by both. His firm made it a standard practice not to take customer accounts of less than $250,000. Despite its high standards, the house was generally reputed to have more than a hundred clients with an aggregate buying power of over $50 million. In addition, the firm did a substantial amount of commission business with the hedge funds. These are relatively small (often under $25 million in assets) pooled funds with a small number of usually affluent partners. Their managers are paid strictly on the basis of performance, sharing in the profits and often receiving an escalating percentage as profits rise.

Cash Argentte's basic approach was not much different from mine. Before a situation appealed to him, he had to see a potential 100% return on his money, and he had to be able to define his downside risks. He also liked "kickers," having had enough experience in this business to realize the overvaluations that can follow when the speculator senses magic.

I outlined the situation to him: ABP was a sound operation; earnings from the building products operations had risen steadily in recent years, but the Magic fiasco had masked this fact. With Magic soon to be disposed of, the real earning power would again be apparent. Efforts would be made to show a steady upward profits progression—growth. There was no present intention of selling off the timber holdings, but the sale of the Michigan lakeside property could be capitalized upon to dramatize the "hidden" values. The research subsidiary was working on some interesting projects that, while not significant in the profit picture, could nurture long-range fantasies.

It was Argentte's kind of situation. He listened and then asked *the* question that was a critical one for him once he had been satisfied with the merits of the situation. "Who owns the stock?" he barked.

I outlined to Argentte the trading history of ABP over the past year. My accumulation campaign was described, but the size of my position (close to 200,000 shares) was understated substantially. Altogether, I summarized, ownership of about half of the outstanding shares could be pinpointed among myself, the directors, and the Founder family.

And here was a problem: There was no indication that there would be a sufficient supply of stock available near the present market price to enable Argentte and his clients to amass a large enough position to make the venture advantageous. Further, liquidity—the ability of the market to absorb either large buy or sell orders without a marked effect on the price of the stock—was also lacking. Liquidity was reputed to be a passion with Argentte, the source of which was attributed to his experience some years ago when he found himself with a few thousand shares of an obscure issue that had to be liquidated quickly. The market was already thin and Argentte's distress-selling knocked it down over 50% in value in one week. A popular story on Wall Street was that a famous art dealer was unsuccessful in an attempt to sell Argentte a Picasso because there were no figures available on how many canvases traded each day, and at what prices.

It was obvious that ABP would not qualify as a vehicle for general use by the clients of Argentte. The total capitalization was not sufficiently large and, even more critical, the floating supply in the hands of traders and short-term investors was decidedly too small. No, I proposed, his participation was to be more limited—limited to the Argentte account itself and those of a very few of its favored customers. Not coincidentally, when these facts were ultimately aired to the Street, this situation would be associated with the best possible sponsorship.

The problem now was to assure Argentte that he would be able to establish a sufficiently large share position to make the endeavor worth the bother. The first part of our agreement was that I would not compete with him for stock for a period of two months. We would not be bidding against each other on the open market, although Argentte, of course, would have to compete with occasional casual buyers attracted to the situation. Thus far, however, there was no indication of any concentrated or substantial buying interest.

Argentte was in a strong bargaining position, and he knew it. He wanted some guarantee that I would not be double-crossing him by unloading my position while his accumulation campaign was in progress. To provide him this assurance, I gave him a "put" on 50,000 shares at $35 a share, 5 points above the current market, for two months. Under the put option, Argentte had the right to deliver to me and force me to buy up to 50,000 shares of ABP stock at 35 for the specified period. Thus, if Argentte were to buy 50,000 shares during the next two months and the stock was not above 35 by the close of that period, he could deliver the stock to me and I would have had to give him 35 a share for up to 50,000 shares, regardless of the then current market price. He was guaranteed against loss during the initial sixty days of the campaign. And, if he were to change his mind about participating in the situation before the period expired, he would have an out. He could simply unload the shares on me.

Simultaneously, Argentte demanded a call on 50,000 shares for nine months, contingent on his not exercising the put. The call option would give Argentte the right to call upon me to deliver to him, within the nine months, 50,000 shares at the set price of $30 a share, regardless of the market price of the stock. This, in effect, would assure him a profit if ABP stock rose above the call price, which was 30, the current market. I considered this too stiff a price to pay —to surrender the potential profit on one-half of the position (100,000) shares that I told him I had in ABP. The market value of such an option, based on prevailing quotations for options on stocks of similar volatility and of comparable price, was about $200,000. We haggled a bit, but Argentte appeared adamant. Finally, I said no deal on these terms, and Argentte accepted a counteroffer of a call on 25,000 shares for six months and ten days, which, under existing tax laws, would enable him to come within the holding period for long-term capital gains treatment.

As the situation now stood, I ran the risk of having to buy 50,000 more shares of ABP stock over the next sixty days. I had little anxiety on this score. If Argentte bought that many shares during the period, it virtually guaranteed that the price would be above the $35 level by the end of the sixty days. If worse came to worst, I would find my position enlarged by a quarter and would have to find other means of obtaining sponsorship. My larger holdings would enable me to offer someone else an incentive to participate in the mark-up campaign.

The call option I gave Argentte would mean a lesser profit for me. In effect, I had given him the potential profit over the six months and ten days on 25,000 shares. This was not too high a price to pay for the benefits I anticipated from Argentte's sponsorship. If ABP advanced to 60 in the period, he would, of course, call the stock from me at the $30 price. This would represent a 30-point profit on each of the 25,000 shares for Argentte, or $750,000. For my remaining 175,000 shares, it would represent a profit of $5.25 million. Argentte was not giving away his Brand of Approval gratis, but it could yet prove a bargain for me.

For the sixty-day period, however, Argentte had me at his mercy. Fortunately, there was little incentive for Argentte to try a bear raid—that is, intentionally forcing the price of the stock down and then exercising the put—and little likelihood of its success in any event. Selling pressure on the stock was negligible, and I was in a position to influence the flow of news from the company, and consequently affect the public attitude toward the stock.

The Argentte house was well known for its close connection with substantial private money, including some of the top Old Money names, the newly rich breed of industrialist and entrepreneur, and some of the hot money from Eastern Mediterranean shipping and oil interests. In addition, its contacts with Washington were excellent, with Argentte himself personally supervising the accounts of some powerful figures in the government. I was confident that Argentte would put this top tier of favored clients in the ABP situation, although their names would never appear on the transfer sheets, the corporation's list of stockholders. The entries would show only the "street name" of Argentte, Mewlaugh and Doe as the purchaser and owner of record. The true owner would never appear in print and would be known only to Argentte, Mewlaugh and Doe and to those whose knowledge of such buying would be beneficial to the performance of the stock.

One mustn't jump to the conclusion, however, that, for example, the involvement of Rockefeller money in a particular situation is a guarantee of its success. By no means, but the probabilities are that Mr. Rockefeller has been able to hire better analytical talent and has better sources of information than Mr. Impecunious Nobody. Moreover, it is not to a manipulator's advantage to "take" a Rockefeller—unless it is for a prodigious sum of money. The Rockefeller type of participant is much too useful to alienate for picayune sums. A Rockefeller's owning ABP stock is something like the Duchess of Windsor's patronizing some obscure couturier who then quickly becomes famous or the Metropolitan Museum's buying an unknown painter who, by definition, is then no longer unknown. That a Rockefeller would own ABP shares is itself a form, and an important one, of sponsorship.

I now withdrew from the market in ABP stock for the agreed sixty days, concentrating on watching the action of the shares and monitoring through Confrer, who had access to them, the entries in the corporation's transfer sheets indicating changes in share ownership. I also watched the pink sheets, which reveal the action of the over-the-counter dealers. After the sharp decline following the Magic fiasco, over-the-counter activity in ABP shares had almost disappeared. The limited turnover and consistent decline of the stock had eliminated its appeal as a trading vehicle. Now, however, Carrion & Co. suddenly appeared as making a market in the stock over the counter. It was a small house that had been used in the past by Argentte to accumulate or distribute stock.

I hypothesized that Carrion would now be acting as a buyer, to accumulate shares for Argentte, and I tested my theory. It proved correct. If, for example, ABP was 29½ bid and 30 offered on the big board, I would call for a quote from Carrion on the stock. He would be bidding 29⅝ and offering stock at 31. He was obviously topping the bid on the floor of the Exchange while offering stock at a higher price than that available on the Stock Exchange. There was no other reason to buy from Carrion, but sellers would find his bid price consistently better than that on the floor. Any broker checking both Carrion and the floor price would sell stock to Carrion and buy on the floor. As Exchange prices fluctuated, the pattern of a higher bid price and higher offering price was maintained. Technically, Carrion was fulfilling his obligation as market maker to make both bids and offers, but no one was likely to take this offer. Consequently, Carrion would remain always as a net buyer.

It was impossible to deduce how many shares Argentte could amass through Carrion over the counter, but anyone with a sizable block to dispose of would find it easier to sell to Carrion than on the floor. The market on the floor was thin and, for example, a 29½–30 market quote was usually 1 by 1, or 2 by 2. If you wanted to sell 1,000 shares on the open market, it might have the effect of dropping the price by a point or more. Carrion, on the other hand, would be willing to take the whole block at only a fraction-of-a-point concession. Buyers, though, would find an extremely thin market on the up side at Carrion, and would thus go to the Exchange floor to do their purchasing.

During this period, there was a gradually spreading awareness of the improved operating situation at the company. This could not be helped. The officers and directors would see the monthly profit and loss statements of the various segments of the business, and those involved in the negotiations to sell the Magic subsidiary were aware of the extent of its losses. They could put two and two together and realize that ABP was making substantial profits and would have to show them once Magic was sold. The accountants who prepared the figures, their secretaries, and their secretaries' boy friends and/or husbands had knowledge of what was happening. The same was true of office boys, janitors, and those who cleaned up the boardroom after directors' meetings. How many would connect the facts with their probable ultimate market significance? Doubtless, some would.

Moreover, I was not the only one who knew that Carrion was often a front for Argentte or that Argentte was interested in the situation and a buyer. Other brokerage houses became aware that something was happening at ABP, but during the sixty-day period Confrer arranged a complete moratorium on information emanating from the company to analysts or brokerage houses. The moment had not arrived for exciting others' interest and enlisting their aid in the campaign. That was to come later, at higher prices.

For now, the objective was to avoid publicity and thus maintain as neutral a market climate as possible to facilitate Argentte in amassing his position. The most important spur to spectator buying, the action of the stock itself, was absent. ABP was holding well in the low to middle 30s, but there was no sharp pickup in volume and, except for its improved ability to absorb offerings, there was nothing to spark trading interest. Thus, there developed no hurry to buy it because, apparently, no one else was in a hurry to buy it.

The sixty days passed and Argentte and I then had lunch. ABP was now selling around 37 and the put on 50,000 shares was about to expire. The only incentive for Argentte to exercise his option now would be that he had changed his mind and had decided to exit from the situation. He could not unload any sizable position, and I assumed that he had bought between 30,000 and 50,000 shares during the period on the open market, from the evidence on the transfer sheets. So, even though the put price was 2 points below the market, he might still choose to exercise the option and force me to take his position at 35.

I had learned from other sources, and without surprise, that Argentte had not relied solely on the information I had given him on the ABP situation. He had researched it himself and was obviously satisfied that this could be a winner. He returned the put contract to me and asked me if I wanted to handle the mark-up phase alone. I told him I would. His inconspicuous, but no longer completely secret, interest was enough assistance for the time being. I would be able to use his help now in establishing the proper relationships with the big retail brokerage houses—those that deal with thousands of small investors and speculators—but I would handle the direct market operations alone.

I now had completed my own position in ABP stock, and a substantial amount was in the right hands (Argentte and select customers). The ABP building products business was going well and I could pretty much determine the final date for disposal of Magic. The next step was the mark-up campaign to get the stock to sell at least 50% higher, while changing the character of the market so that it would eventually be able to absorb up to 200,000 shares at those higher prices.

13 The Concept

Paralleling classical and somewhat satanic conceptions of the market cycle, the accumulation phase had now been completed. The mark-up phase was next. Those who follow the "they" school of a consciously manipulated market cycle describe the stages as (1) Accumulation, (2) Mark-up, (3) Distribution, and (4) Mark-down, proceeding back to Accumulation and a repetition of the whole cycle. Of course, the pontificating market letter writers on Wall Street who habitually use these terms suffer from a profound identity crisis. By the prevailing outsiders' view, these brokers' hucksters should be considered a constituent of the "they's" who impel markets, rather than the "we's" who simply react once markets begin to move.

It is not out of humility that these "they's" consider themselves to be humble "I's" or "we's"; the attitude simply reflects their bondage to the prevalent superstition that a consensus of investment Supermen determines stock market movements. By definition, the "they" Supermen cannot be specifically identified. The most a "we" or an "I" can hope for is to follow by sheerest accident or good fortune the same course of action as the "they's," buying when "they" do (and not from "them") and selling when "they" do (and not to "them"), trusting in "their" expertise that "I" or "we" will find our buying cheap and our selling dear.

In the case of ABP stock, there *was* a "they," and I am pleased to identify that "they" as me. And in this instance, the market strategy was to follow the traditional accumulation, mark-up, and distribution cycle. I had bought my 200,000 shares of ABP at the bottom. I was able to buy them at the bottom because I had made the bottom. I had been willing and able to absorb all the stock offered in the high teens and the low twenties.

If I had changed my mind after taking my position in the stock and had decided to buy no more, perhaps ABP would have gone lower and all of my stock shown an unrealized loss. Then the Street savants would have spoken of the action of the stock during the period of my buying as "distribution," since it would have been followed by a decline in price. But since, in fact, an advance followed substantial buying in ABP, the retrospective definition is accumulation.

In this instance there was literally accumulation—one buyer had accumulated the holdings of hundreds of mostly small stockholders during a period of several months. This is the only sense in which the popularly misused term "accumulation" can have any real meaning. Often, you will find that the number of shareholders in a particular large-capitalization company has contracted sharply in a period of one or two years. This means that the size of the average share position of stockholders is increasing, which supports the inference that the small investor is selling out to persons of greater affluence. Since a basic premise on Wall Street (and perhaps in the whole country) is that the intellectual capacity of money is directly related to its size, one can assume that the "accumulators" will eventually prove to have been "smart."

The accumulation phase in ABP having been accomplished, I had only laid the groundwork and completed the first step toward my ultimate goal: the resale of my shareholdings at a profit. This final phase would be distribution of my large holdings to a vast number of smaller stock buyers at higher prices. The problem now was achieving higher prices—the mark-up that would be prologue to the distribution. One method, of course, would be to continue buying the stock until it reached my price objective. But there was no way of knowing how much more stock I would have to absorb on the way, say, to $60. I would be running the risk of having to carry a substantially larger position, and raising my average price to a level that, even assuming I would ultimately unload at $60 a share, would preclude a large enough profit to compensate for the risks involved in the campaign.

I was willing to buy some additional stock to help in the mark-up, but my strategy now was to enlist the buying power of others in propelling the stock higher. My agreement with Argentte was the first step in that direction. The next component in the mark-up phase was to create a second tier—the next-to-the-inner circle—who would be willing purchasers of ABP stock on what they considered to be ABP's own merits.

Of course, in allowing others to board the bandwagon, I was running the risk that they would try to decamp later on, when I would be unloading my position. But there would be two ways to minimize this risk. One would be to have created a sufficiently broad and active market in ABP stock that it could absorb sizable liquidation later on at higher prices. The second would be to cause the merits of the shares to appear so formidable that holders would be unwilling to part with them even at much higher prices.

The identity of this second tier of professional investors varies, depending on the characteristics of the particular stock. If we were concerned with a high-grade issue of blue-chip quality, institutional investors such as pension funds, insurance companies, and mutual funds would be the unwitting participants in the mark-up stage, and usually in the distribution phase as well. High technology or concept issues are in a class by themselves. Here, creation of an active market, combined with a steady progression of "mystery non-news"

—usually in the form of obscure products or technology that mean nothing in terms of generating sales or earnings but are sufficiently mysterious to excite the imagination of speculators—and a steady progression of earnings gains frequently suffices to enlist enough traders to provide the mark-up and create the liquid market that will facilitate subsequent distribution.

But ABP was a hybrid, a special situation. To interest institutions at this stage of the game, before there was more convincing evidence of a turnaround in the form of a protracted period of improving earnings, would be difficult, except for a few small, imaginative funds. ABP was a special breed of investment that required a certain breed of buyer. There were some fairly sophisticated brokerage houses that specialized in buying into special situations for themselves and a few large customers. If I could attract their interest, the mark-up would present little difficulty.

Confrer, now firmly in control of investor relations, mapped out a program to whet the investment appetites of these second-tier houses. A series of luncheons was arranged for partners of these firms. Founder was intensively briefed on his presentation, the gist of which was that ABP had made a mistake with Magic Transistor, and now had, for all practical purposes, disposed of this admittedly unprofitable operation. To provide a clearer view of its basic earning power in the past few years, these luncheon audiences were presented with a restatement of ABP's results, excluding Magic. A restatement is a common accounting device used to present results had a specific operation not been present. Without Magic, the ABP earnings record was quite respectable, revealing a reasonably steady progression of profits, punctuated occasionally by slight setbacks due to cyclical economic factors.

In addition, Founder emphasized the new orientation of the present management—more toward vertical integration,

with emphasis on higher-margin products for ultimate sale
to the consumer, so that eventually the company would provide everything for the home, from lumber to lighting fix-
tures. Aided by its already broad distribution network, and
benefiting from the cost advantages of vertical integration
from raw material to finished product, ABP could prove a
formidable competitor in all areas it entered.

Furthermore, ABP's financial position was strong, and
the balance sheet included many understated assets. More
information was provided relating to the sale of the Michigan
lakeside property. Founder indicated that timberland holdings were carried on the books at an average of only $4 an
acre but couldn't be replaced for fifty times that figure. A
quick extrapolation suggested hidden assets worth $100
million or more. Restrained allusions were also made to accelerated progress by the chemical research subsidiary, working on some exciting new products.

In presenting a story to professional investors, the packag-
ing is fully as important as the product. Wall Street has a
habit of counting the same tricks more than once. Thus, although a growth record itself is the result of capable management, the Street is willing to pay an additional bonus for
good management on top of the premium for past growth—
although one is a function of the other. Founder was well
schooled in his mission. It was essential that he instill confidence and portray the dynamic, imaginative professional
manager who knows where he has been (including the mistakes along the route), where he is going, and who has the
talents and drive to achieve his objectives.

There was much "concept" fodder in the presentation. The
broad picture—beloved of all Wall Street—was that of an
asset-rich company just now beginning to realize a satisfactory return on its invested capital. Profit margins would be
the key to results in the future. The company plan was ultimately to bring ten cents of each sales dollar down to net

profit, and to obtain an overall return on capital of 20%. Where was the company going? That question had to be anticipated, for the personnel-manager psychology that requires a "formulation of long-range personal objectives" was not alien to the Street. For ABP to make progressively more money was not enough; we had to present a concept that would at least temporarily immortalize ABP shares in the imagination of investors.

The concept was simple, but one that could activate the imagination of the most profit-oriented investor. Founder cited figures that showed that 1,000 board feet of lumber, if used for making wooden sidings for residential construction, would ultimately produce only $100 in profits. The same raw materials turned into specialty interior paneling could mean $1,000 in profits. All that was necessary was an upgrading of the product line! This was to be the key to dynamic gains in profits in the future. The necessary ingredients for this upgrading program were substantial capital, manufacturing know-how, and an efficient and broad marketing and distributing organization—and ABP had all of these. In addition, the potential of the residential building market itself was not to be underestimated. The industry's manufacturing and marketing techniques were archaic, giving the dynamic management at ABP a chance to exploit the limitless opportunities for innovation in this seemingly prosaic field.

All of this fired the imagination, but the professional audiences also wanted something tangible in the way of earnings in the immediate future. And Founder could oblige them. Internal company projections were of profits for the year of approximately $4 a share, after a full allowance for the normal corporate tax rate. Because of the Magic fiasco, ABP now had a sizable tax loss carryforward. But ABP management, "although not conservative in operations, is very conservative in its accounting" and consequently had decided to accrue (although it would not pay) taxes at a normal rate.

Even the most skeptical of those who heard the presentation considered the stock, now around 40, to be quite reasonably valued. Some were favorably impressed with the picture of management and with the company's prospects, and a few were genuinely excited, viewing ABP as a real bargain. No dramatic developments were imminent that would cause them to stampede to buy the stock, but sufficient interest had been generated so that I could anticipate a fairly steady stream of buying by some accounts of these brokerage houses. Their demand would absorb stock around the present price level and perhaps move it into the high 40s. From then on, my own market maneuvers and a steady stream of good news from the company would be needed to give the stock upward momentum.

14 Mark-Up

It was now late spring, time to report operating results for the first quarter. ABP shares were trading in the low 40s, holding well in response to the second-tier buying, most of which had been done with sufficient deliberation to keep the stock from running away. In contrast to a loss in the last two quarters of the preceding year, the company now reported a profit of $0.75 a share in the first quarter. The $0.75 figure was after a provision for taxes accruable at a 55% rate. This was well above the rate the corporation would normally pay, but the excessive allowance was designed to provide a cushion. If results in any particular subsequent quarter did not reach our projections, the tax reserve could be reduced, thereby boosting reported earnings. Managements of most large, complex companies not only manage operations but also manage earnings to a considerable extent on an interim basis. Unlike cumulative results for the full year, profits for any particular quarter are susceptible to highly subjective, judgmental factors. The trend was the important thing; it was essential that a steady progression be reported and that we did not disappoint the expectations of the Street.

On release of the earnings, the stock attracted some trading interest, moving easily to the high 40s. I immediately shorted a few thousand shares, in part to broaden the market in the

107

stock and in part to check the rise. Too much too soon would invite too much profit taking. Some buyers who had picked up the stock in the high 20s and low 30s were happy to see a relatively quick 30%–50% return on their investment, and they sold. Combined with my offerings, the supply of stock was enough to knock it back to the 40 level, where I reentered the market as a steady buyer. I was covering the short position established only days before in the high 40s and was again contributing to a more orderly price continuity and to a broader market for the stock.

The appearance of consistent buying support at 40 bolstered the confidence of those who had been buyers in the high 30s and low 40s. More important, my activity helped to maintain a higher level of average daily volume. ABP trading turnover was now close to 3,000 shares a day—not an enormous amount, but a volume reassuring to traders and investors accustomed to dealing in thousands of shares. Moreover, orderly and less volatile action would reassure long-term holders who only a year before had seen the stock drop to below 20 from above 60, and who might now be prone to seize an excuse to get out. The action of the stock was calculated to inhibit any sense of urgency to sell.

The key to my strategy now was to maintain a steady flow of moderately favorable news and gradually attract more interest. With the stock holding around 40, management announced that an increase in the dividend would be considered at the next directors' meeting. This didn't spur any sudden surge of buying, but it was an encouraging bit of news. A steady flow of goodies for the shareholders would help to tilt decisions away from selling, and it was as important at this stage to keep offerings by existing holders off the market as to encourage new investors to buy.

A few weeks later the board met, and true to expectations, a boost in the cash dividends, to $0.25 quarterly, was announced. Simultaneously, the company release stated that, while current earning power would support a materially higher cash payout, management intended to retain a greater proportion of profits to use for expansion. This was part of the new growth image. The release continued that, "Reflecting the directors' awareness that the company is being operated for the benefit of shareholders" (a charming fiction), a stock dividend of 5% was declared. This largesse was a surprise and more than counterbalanced any disappointment over the small size of the cash disbursement. The stock responded well, aided by the desire of many traders and speculators to buy before the 5% dividend was paid, so that they would be entitled to receive it. The stock stabilized in the middle 40s.

Summer arrived and it was soon time for the second-quarter report. Seasonal factors tended to inflate sales and profits in that period, and ABP actually earned $2.50 a share before taxes in the three months. But nothing was to be gained by reporting such an astonishingly high figure; it was enough that the earnings recovery was solidly in place. The more prudent course, again, was to conserve some of this profit for later, in the event operating results were disappointing. So the rate of corporate income tax accrual was lifted to about 58% and a reserve was set up for "contingencies"—the net result of which was to bring the final earnings figure down to around $1.10 a share. With $1.85 now reported for the first half, and the second half traditionally the stronger one, earnings projections of $4 a share started to look decidedly conservative.

The stream of good news and the impressive earnings reports were beginning to attract considerably more attention from individual investors and among brokerage houses. The stock was continually on the new highs list, itself a formidable bit of point-of-purchase advertising. Everyone who had bought the stock within the past year now had a profit, at least on paper, and thus was a happy owner, a public relations plus. More and more persons were interested in ABP, and it was becoming a suitable subject for brokerage house analysis and recommendation.

Security analysts began to call on the company. While they were told nothing specific on the value of the timberland or on the progress of the chemical subsidiary, they were given projections of earnings of $3.50 a share for the year, which they were assured would prove conservative. Since the first-half figures were already out, many analysts felt the $3.50 figure to be too conservative and preferred to come forth with their own projections, which ran as high as the $4.25–$4.75 area. With many security analysts, it is essential that management provide substantial help and guidance in reaching earnings estimates. Frequently, an analyst will avoid coverage of a company if he does not feel he can rely on management to help with such estimates, but ABP was cordial and cooperative. The company's long-range plans for expansion, growth, and upgrading of the product line were revealed with polish and conviction. An ugly duckling at 20, ABP became comely, if not glamorous, in the 50s.

At around 50, the stock was no bargain. On a historical basis and in relation to stocks of comparable companies in the same industry, ABP shares were reasonably valued at approximately 12 times earnings (after provision for taxes) estimated for the year. It is rare, however, that a stock enjoying a substantial measure of investment or speculative interest remains in an area of reasonable valuation. A former favorite fallen from grace often sinks too low, receding to a level that represents a statistical bargain. But when a board-room darling is still in vogue, the high price of the charms of ownership will often bear only the remotest relationship to rational standards of security valuation.

Bear markets, before they have run their course, are typified ultimately by undervaluation. Stocks are simply not wanted, and price is irrelevant. The lower the price, the larger the community of unhappy owners and the more likely that additional selling, rather than buying, will be inspired by further drops in price. Always in the background is the omniscient "they" theory—the stock is so cheap because "they" know something bad that "we" don't. The converse, of course, prevails at bull market peaks, when overvaluation is the rule. Stocks are preferred to cash, and since stocks are going up and therefore will go higher, the price one pays now is immaterial.

Once again, one must remember the similarity to an auction, with both buyers and sellers competing. Just as at any auction, the price at which a stock (or an art object) is knocked down depends on the anxiousness of the prospective owner to own the chattel rather than to have cash or alternative chattels. And, of course, what you are willing to pay at an auction is largely dependent upon what others are willing to pay at that same moment. Maybe you thought the Chippendale chair was worth $200 when you saw it on exhibit the day before the auction. During the sale, perhaps some others were willing to pay $400 for it—maybe "they" knew something you didn't or maybe "their" judgment was better than yours. You wind up paying $500 for the chair and feel you have a bargain—until you get home and the frenzied atmosphere of the auction market gives way to calm appraisal and, perhaps, recriminations.

Auction fever had not yet touched ABP stock, but a good part of the mark-up had already been accomplished for me earlier by professional buyers, as well as by some brokerage houses and, more recently, by the general public responding to the earnings reports and the dividend increase. But the stock was now only "fairly valued," and fair valuation was not my objective. There were elements in the picture of glamour and mystery that could result in substantial overvaluation if properly handled—and this was what I was shooting for.

The stock had now settled in the 45–50 range. Trading

volume had picked up to around 5,000 shares a day. I continued my policy of helping to broaden the market and maintain a more orderly performance by selling shares at 50 and rebuying them at around 45. Those who watched the action of the stock soon recognized the pattern. The result was heightened buying interest around 45–46, while those willing to sell around 50 were gradually taken out of their positions, and their number diminished.

This lateral action continued for about two more months. A constant stream of insignificant but agreeable news was released by the company. Each time a new machine was bought for a plant, there was a report of progress in the "modernization program" at such-and-such facility. Founder continued to make occasional speeches before professional groups. The image of business statesmanship was now established, but needed sustained nourishment.

15 A Little

Bear Trap

The action of the stock—zigzagging aimlessly in the 45–50 area—had attracted the attention of some chartists, who now were awaiting a breakout from this trading range. That would be the signal for them to hop on the bandwagon and participate in a new move for the stock. A breakout for chartists is a move out of a well-defined trading range. It can be either a buy or a sell signal, since it is believed to herald the beginning of a sizable move in the direction of the breakout.

The theory behind breakouts is simplicity itself. In the instance of ABP, for example, one can picture a struggle between the supply of stock available for sale at 50—large enough to turn back each advance—and the demand for stock at 45, which stops each decline. We have an evenly matched supply-demand situation. Eventually, either the supply of stock at 50 would be absorbed and the stock would begin rising above that level until supply once again satisfied demand, or the demand for stock would fall off before the supply at 50 was absorbed. If the latter happened, the stock would falter

113

and swamp the support at 45 and then decline to a new, lower level where another supply-demand equilibrium would evolve. The longer the stock stays in the 45–50 area, the more dynamic the momentum provided by the ultimate shift in the supply-demand balance is likely to be, and the larger the ensuing move up—or down.

I figured that once all the sellers willing to take 50 had disposed of their stock, ABP could move up easily. Everyone who had wanted out at that price level would be accommodated and a worthwhile advance could follow before those who wouldn't take 50 would come to market with their shares. The extent of the move and the supply en route would, of course, also depend on the price objectives of those who had been buying around 45. Obviously, however, most of those who won't sell at 50 are not going to sell at 51 or 52. So it was reasonable in this case to expect a gain of 5 points or more to follow a breakout.

I was anxious to limit the amount of offerings that would eventually be made right above 50. This is one reason that I did not earlier break the stock out myself, by buying perhaps 10,000 shares in the 50–51 area to get the move started. To limit the probable supply right above 50, I wanted to shake out some of the short-term traders, leaving intact only those who had sufficient conviction that they wouldn't leap to sell just above 50. Simultaneously, I hoped to attract some short sellers who would in effect provide additional supplies of stock at bargain prices and inadvertently help fuel a more dynamic runaway move in the stock later on.

To achieve these objectives, I decided to try to cause a down-side breakout—a decline in the stock below the 45 level, where consistent support had appeared in the past. My own experience with short sellers is that there are two distinct categories, the professional and the amateur. The amateur will short a stock simply because it has risen "too much." He is closely related to the fellow who buys a stock solely because it is sharply down from its high and therefore is considered a bargain. Both these strategies—that of shorting a stock just because it has advanced a lot, or of buying it because it is selling at such a large discount from its peak price —can be disastrous.

The professional short seller usually employs a completely different strategy, with his prime orientation toward fundamental business conditions. He will often sell short a stock that has already declined substantially, if it is still a deteriorating situation. He realizes that a stock that has had a substantial decline is in a weak technical position: There are too many owners who have unrealized losses and who constitute an overhanging supply of stock available for sale. That situation will usually preclude any major rally for the stock.

If the professional does short in this type of situation, he will have plenty of warning if his judgment is going to be proved wrong. The stock is not going to explode on the up side, and if it does begin to act too well, he will be able to cover his position without having to compete for stock with amateur shorts stampeding to cover their positions. Probably a major part of professional short selling is done on superior information or greater comprehension of adverse developments affecting a company or an industry.

The professional short seller will also short a rising stock if he feels the buying is misinformed, or that demand for the stock has been stimulated by specific news developments. Arch Adams, one of the more successful of the old-time professional traders, has realized an excellent return for some years from this strategy. If a stock has had a 10% or larger advance within the two weeks before announcement of a stock split or large divided increase (and there have been no other favorable developments), Adams shorts the stock immediately on the announcement of the split or dividend boost. His rationale is that the insiders and their friends have already bought the stock and caused it to rise, in anticipation of the public's response to this development.

The better informed will immediately sell on the news to

the public. Many of the amateurs who buy on the news expect to make a quick profit by selling at a higher price a day or two later. They are obviously operating on the Greater Fool Theory—that some other idiot will bail them out at a higher price. However, if stock movements are supposed to be anticipatory, why should a stock advance after the good news is out? The old adage "sell on the news" means simply that this is the moment when you will get the highest price and the broadest interest in your stock—the best time to unload it.

So, my strategy was to cause a down-side breakout below the 45 support level, shaking out the uncertain holders and short-term scalpers, reducing the supply available once the stock moved up past the 50 area, and trapping some short sellers. Since the stock had now traded in the 45–50 range for almost two months and volume had expanded to close to 4,000 shares daily, I was able to assume there would be substantial stop-loss orders just below 45.

Stop-loss (really stop-sell) orders are a device usually employed by traders to limit their losses automatically in the event of a decline in a stock. Stop-buy orders are used to jump automatically on the bandwagon when a stock begins to rise. The traders who had watched ABP fluctuate between 45 and 50 and who owned the stock could put in an order at 44½ —a stop-loss order so that they would automatically sell their stock if it broke down out of the trading range. Thus, if ABP receded to 44½ the order immediately became one to sell at the market. If, at that moment, there was active buying interest in the stock, the order might be executed within a small fraction of the 44½ price.

But a mass of stop-loss orders at the same point would mean that a substantial number of shares would be suddenly offered "at the market" and the orders themselves could cause a drop of a few points. Conversely, the trader who didn't own ABP and had watched the action between 45 and 50 might put a stop-buy at 50½—which would become an order to buy at the market when the stock rose to 50½. He would be calculating that a move past 50, above the supply area, would mark the beginning of a sizable advance and he would automatically want to join in.

I doubted if there would be much in the way of orders to buy the stock right under 45; anyone willing to pay 43 or 44 would probably have already gotten impatient and either have bought at 45 or turned to other issues. Thus, it might take a 3- or 5-point drop to attract bargain hunters.

But I had to be careful not to allow the stock to perform so erratically and poorly as to disenchant the long-term holders and those serious investors who had bought in recent months. They had to be reassured, and remain willing to hold on to their stock, while the short-term traders were being thoroughly routed.

I chose Thursday as the day for the shakeout. The stock was now at the lower end of the 45–50 range, having traded between 45½ and 46½ the preceding day on turnover of 3,600 shares. Trading volume was about 1,500 shares the first three hours of the Thursday session and the quote was 45¾–46 at one o'clock.

I was aiming to attract the notice of the lunchtime boardroom habitués. I tested the size of the market by offering 600 shares for sale at 45¾. Only 200 were taken and the quote became 45½–45¾. I withdrew the 400 balance at 45¾ and reoffered 700 at 45½. Only 100 were taken and the quote became 45⅛–45½. I withdrew the offering of 600 at 45½ and immediately offered 800 at 45⅛. Three hundred were taken at 45⅛ and the market then became 45–45⅛, 1,900 by 500. The round-number psychology at work again—45 was attractive to a number of potential buyers.

It was now a few minutes after one and the boardroom voyeurs had seen a sequence of ABP transactions at progressively lower prices, and on expanding volume. The 45 area was one of key support, and some traders became nervous as it approached that level. The stock traded 200 at 45, 200 at 45, then two 100-share lots at 45. I checked the size of the market again. Most of the orders at 45 had been withdrawn —there was now only a bid for 200 shares at that price.

This is typical of the bargain hunter's psychology: The trader who watched ABP move up to 50 says if it ever gets back down to 45, he will buy it. He puts in his order at 45. As ABP approaches that price, he begins thinking maybe he can get it cheaper. So he drops his price to 40. When the stock declines to 41, he drops his bid to 37. It winds up that he never buys the stock on the way down; perhaps he never really wanted to own it in the first place. But when the stock turns up again, he raises his limit order—but it is still *under* the market. Finally, when the stock hits 70, he gives up in disgust and buys it at the market, which turns out to be a hair from the top.

It happens similarly with the profit-taker. He may have bought ABP at 30. "I'll sell it when it goes to 40. A 10-point profit is enough." ABP moves to 38 and the owner says, "I want 45." ABP moves to 44, he wants 50, and so on. He won't sell on the way up. So, when the stock begins to decline he begins dropping his sell point, but it always remains *above* the market. Finally, he sells at the market when ABP again hits 30—right where he started. It reminds me of the cynic's interpertation of GTC orders. Are they "good till canceled" or are they "good till close" orders?

The buy orders at 45 quickly disappeared when it was likely that they would be filled. Another 200 shares went by at 45 and then there was a pause. Five minutes later there were a few strings of 200 and 300 shares down to 44—and then the deluge. The stock began to pour out below 44, at which point I put in a few orders to buy at the market. The stock hit 43 and I got around 1,500 shares, almost all in 100-share lots at 43⅛ and from twelve different sellers. This was obviously short selling. When you see that a stock has fallen suddenly and sharply on fairly heavy volume and then stabilizes at some point on ⅛ upticks, the probabilities are that these transactions reflect execution of orders to short at the market, usually by 100-share-lot traders.

My buying stabilized the price by about two-thirty, and the stock was holding near 43 at the close. Then the bargain hunters, who remembered that the stock had traded 3 points higher earlier in the session, came in as buyers. Their demand helped to give the stock a firmer tone and its apparent ability to hold its new, lower price level evidently dissuaded any additional traders from liquidating for the time being. The close was fractionally above 43. Turnover had reached 16,000 shares, the highest in recent memory, and ABP was down 3 points for the day.

The opening on Friday was larger than usual—2,500 shares at 41½—as selling by traders slightly overcame buying by bargain hunters. I bought scattered 100-share lots all at upticks, hoping that I would be buying from short sellers. Quoting ABP during the day would reveal offerings usually ⅛ above the last sale, and only of 100 shares, indicating short selling.

The action had now served my purposes. Weak holders, who would have been only too willing to sell at 51 or so, had been shaken out. But the damage had not been so severe that long-term investors were worried. Moreover, I had now presented a perfect chart picture to lure more shorts.

16 Celebrity Status

Over the weekend, one of the more venturesome trading advisory services recommended ABP as a short and as an outright sale. The opening was 1,500 shares at 42¾, down ½ from the Friday closing. The quote was then 42¾–42⅞, 3 by 2. I took the 200 shares at ⅞, and this was followed by 300 at ¾ and 100 at ⅝. Then the quote was ⅝ by ¾, 1 by 3. I bought the 300 at ¾. I stepped away from the market and there were no more trades for a few minutes. Then two 100-share lots at ¾ were offered, again suggesting there was no long stock being offered, only shorts.

During the balance of Monday afternoon I bought about 3,000 shares, all between 42½ and 43 from about twenty-two different sellers. At about 3 P.M., ABP was selling fractionally above 43 when the scalpers who had bought at the opening in the hopes of a 2-point rebound had to throw in the towel. I made no attempt to support the market right after three o'clock and the scalpers' selling dropped ABP down to 42. This action emboldened the shorts, and I bought another 1,000 shares in the final fifteen minutes, all on upticks just above 42.

At the closing bell, ABP had traded nearly 14,000 shares and was down ½ point from the Friday close. The stock was still below the 45–50 area and I felt that additional shorts could be attracted to the situation. On Tuesday, the stock opened at 42½ on only 700 shares and I immediately began to peck away at the short offerings. I moved the stock up to 45 around noon. The shorts were again emboldened by appearances that the supply at 45 was still proving insurmountable. Some additional short offerings were made under 44 and I absorbed them. The stock turned dull during lunch. I was waiting to make my move.

It was now apparent to me that no large amounts of stock were being offered by investors, but that shorts were providing most of the supply. The drop below 45 had shaken out some holders, but these were now out of the way. So I was ready to spring my bear trap: My objective was to move ABP back safely up into the 45–50 area, ensuring that all the recent shorts would have an unrealized loss, and simultaneously reassuring any wavering investors that they should hold on to their positions.

Around three o'clock I began my buying in earnest. I was willing to take up to 15,000 shares to get ABP securely in the 45–50 area. The more rapidly it could be accomplished, the less supply I would have to absorb from serious investors. Once ABP was again trading around 50, the decline retrospectively would seem to them to have been a random occurrence, without significance.

The appearance of a few 1,000-share upticks on the tape did the trick. The shorts were unnerved and immediately stopped offering stock, and the scalpers joined the bandwagon on the buy side. The floor traders also sensed the trap, and suddenly 500-share lots were commonplace. Floor trader A would buy 500 shares at 46, then sell them to floor trader B at 46¼, who would sell the 500 to floor trader C at 46⅜, who would sell the 500 shares in smaller lots to boardroom watchers who now bought their 100 shares each "at the market." ABP closed with a flourish at 48½—and I had had to buy only 7,000 shares, all under 45, during the session.

The stock remained active in the 47–49 range for the next two sessions, with the shorts still selling on balance, although a few who decided to cut their losses brought in their shares to close out positions. Volume then subsided but had now reached a daily average of around 10,000 shares. The time had arrived for the next mark-up. Late in the session, I placed an order to take all offerings up to 49½, calculating that this would start a run through the 50 area, setting off some stop-buy orders as well as triggering some short covering.

It took only about 4,000 shares of my buying to do the trick. The stock really began to boil. The floor traders again sensed something going on. They could see the stop-buy point being gunned for and they rolled into action. Strings of 1,000 and 2,000 shares started to go over the ticker tape above 49 and, as ABP hit a supply vacuum right above 50, the stock ran to 52.

The daylighters—that intrepid and profoundly suicidal breed of trader who expects to enter into and close a transaction in one day, and make a profit despite high transaction costs and intense competition from professional traders who are not hampered by commission expenses—helped by hopping on the bandwagon once ABP touched 50. Some shorts panicked at the move to a new high and covered, so it was an easy matter for ABP to rise to 54.

I supplied a fair amount of the stock that traded above 50. My basic strategy was to retain my position at 150,000 shares for the big killing. Interim control over the stock's performance could be accomplished by adding or selling shares as immediate circumstances dictated. I was a net seller of about 2,000 shares thus far during the session. I anticipated that the daylighters would shortly come in as sellers and I wanted to be able to buy from them in order for ABP to close on a strong note. ABP quickly eased on the daylighters' selling, falling back to 52 by shortly after three o'clock. The setback attracted a few shorts; the stock settled momentarily at 52, and I bought 3,000 shares at the market in the final minutes of trading, to close the stock at a new high of 54½.

In the space of about two weeks, ABP had evolved from an illiquid bore into an attractive trading vehicle. Total turnover had reached 45,000 shares in the session ABP hit 54½—the highest level since the crash days of over a year before. There were perhaps 20,000 short sales in the situation, all representing unrealized losses. Of the 45,000-share turnover, perhaps 15,000 shares ended up in different hands at the close of the session from the day before. The rest was traded from A to B to C to A.

The market had broadened substantially and ABP had acquired a combination of volatility and liquidity that made the issue attractive to traders and large investors alike. The manner in which the bear trap had been sprung did not escape the notice of the more sophisticated tape watchers, and now ABP was surrounded with the priceless aura of having attracted "smart money."

A large amount of ABP shares had been dislodged from heretofore permanent holders over the preceding months, but part of this had gone into new, also long-term–oriented, hands. Of paramount importance, a substantial supply of stock for trading had become available. And the floor traders had seen the possibilities in the situation.

This was a decisive change in character for ABP. The floating supply of a stock has a vital bearing on its action and its attraction, but often it has little to do with the total number of outstanding shares. DuPont, for example, with its then 40-plus-million-share capitalization, was for years a notably thin and erratic market performer, prone to relatively wide price gyrations on very small turnover, a phenomenon due to so much of the stock being "locked up" in safe-deposit boxes and not in the trading supply. Thus, as a trading vehicle, the stock had no following. Its character changed consid-

erably as a consequence of the 50%mark-down in the price
of the shares in 1965–66; the dislodging of so much
locked-up stock created a broader and more interesting trading market. Conversely, many speculative issues with less
than a million shares outstanding can support average daily
turnover of 25,000–50,000 shares. In these situations, the
bulk of the outstanding shares are readily available for
trading.

Often, the capitalization of a speculative favorite will turn
over a number of times in one year. Thus, XYZ, with an outstanding capitalization of 1 million shares, will have turnover of 5 million shares during the year. This doesn't mean
that you have had four completely new sets of owners during
the year—by no means. Perhaps 80% of the shares never
changed hands, but the other 20% changed hands dozens of
times during the year. Total turnover of 5 million shares *can*
mean 200,000 shares going from A to B to C to A, *etc.*, 25
times.

Thus, since so many investors never disturb their stock
portfolios, it is frequently those traders dealing with a small
fraction of the capitalization—that small visible part of the
iceberg—who determine the price action of a stock. The same
is true of the market in general: Over short swings, it is the
traders who make the trend. Over long swings, we all know
our fate.

ABP was now well into the mark-up phase, having approached its historical high and having advanced over 100%
from my average purchase price. A lot of stale stock that had
languished in the hands of unhappy holders had been dislodged, and ABP had developed a strong trading interest. It
now enjoyed a broad and liquid market. ABP had gained
popularity and momentum; with a little luck, I could now get
it moving like a fireball. The explosive phase of the mark-up
stage was to come, and after that the critical period of distribution. I still had to unload close to $10 million worth of
stock.

17 Stardom

A star had been born. ABP got top billing on its 45,000-share day, appearing on the list of most actively traded issues on the New York Stock Exchange, as well as among issues making new highs for the year. Turnover was now running over 10 times the average daily trading volume of just a few months before.

ABP now had a devoted following. Indeed, since the stock had climbed near an all-time high and virtually every owner had a paper profit, it had developed quite a fan club. There was still some stale supply in the 60s from unfortunate investors (*sic*) who had bought over a year ago on the run-up misinspired by euphoria over the Magic Transistor acquisition, but their number was small. Everyone loves a winner, and ABP was definitely a winner. The only losers were the shorts, who by now were fairly numerous—all trapped at materially lower prices and vulnerable to stampede psychology under the proper circumstances.

The ABP executive offices were besieged by calls from analysts of brokerage houses seeking interviews with management. Simultaneously, those financial reporters for newspapers who have the impossible task of finding simple cause-and-effect explanations for what are often only random price movements became frequent callers for assistance.

All enquiries were directed to the public relations expert

we had hired, who had received options to buy sizable amounts of the stock. He was to give the critical figures freely: the projection of $4 a share after provision for taxes. He was also to be cooperative in revealing the exact profit received from the sale of land the previous year. Nothing was said to preclude any inference one might choose to make about the value of other timberland holdings. An absolute denial, also gratuitous, was made that the chemical research subsidiary was on the verge of startling technological break-throughs. True, work was continuing on techniques to speed the growth of trees, especially seedlings, and on forest gene-tics to isolate a strain of supertrees, but the company had "absolutely no comment at this time on the state of developments."

By a stroke of luck, a major oil company had some time before undertaken a geological exploration program in Mis-sissippi adjacent to substantial timber holdings held by the Southern division of ABP. The oil concern wanted to include ABP's property in its geological survey and obtained the right to begin drilling on ABP acreage if its findings warranted. ABP refused comment on rumors that it also was con-sidering a drilling program on some of its property and would give out no details of the agreement with the oil com-pany. The less specificity, the more fantasy and more fertile ground for favorable rumors.

The stock was now performing well on its own momentum and it was gaining a substantial backing from Wall Street brokerage houses. The continuing flow of positive, although prosaic, news was maintained. The dividend was raised to $0.35 quarterly at the next directors' meeting, and stock-holders were advised that "despite continued high capital needs for maintaining the growth and expansion of your com-pany, management remains fully aware of shareholders' rights to participate in the progress of their enterprise." Could further boosts and stock dividends be far behind?

Having achieved stardom—constantly on the new highs list, frequently recommended, and now emerging as a respectable investment vehicle—the stock began to evoke greater interest among mutual funds. The Broad Wall Fund, among the larger in the so-called aggressive category, dispatched an analyst for a three-day sojourn with company officials. This lengthy visit gave him ample opportunity to view much of the timberlands, factories, and distribution centers. Whether this firsthand examination provided any additional insight into the business is highly problematical, but some institutions assign first priority to being thorough rather than right. As long as an intensive analysis has been done, it is almost irrelevant whether or not the final investment decision proves profitable. Escaping criticism or lawsuits for insufficient depth of research is the prime motive. This is why brokerage houses that cater primarily to institutions habitually turn out the most verbose and tedious analyses. The mere length of the report allows the portfolio manager to feel confident of the final decision, even though he may lack a genuine comprehension of the stock or industry.

The Broad Wall analyst was given what seemed like complete cooperation, particularly in satisfying his intense curiosity about the sale of the timberlands the previous year. He was told that the parcel represented only a fraction of the company's holdings and was sold only because management believed the capital could be better employed elsewhere in the business, especially for research, development, and product-upgrading programs. The company had a larger captive supply of lumber than it needed and in fact was a net seller of lumber to others. Management would be responsive to other offers for land if the price and timing were advantageous. Timberland was becoming more scarce and thus progressively more valuable, so time favored ABP as a seller. Some interesting offers had been received, but there were no plans for "immediate sales" of additional land.

Today and next year, however, were not sufficient for the

portfolio managers of the Broad Wall Fund, religiously committed to long-term investment. The analyst was anxious to know "where ABP was going." In response to this enquiry, he was treated to a confidential look at the company's ten-year master plan—an impressive, articulate fantasy created by one of the most expensive and prestigious management consultant firms in the business. The map of the future was filled with pompous conceptualizations and projections: ABP was to evolve into a more broadly based supplier to all phases of the construction and paper-consuming industries. Ultimately, branded consumer items offering wider margins and more dynamic growth were to become a dominant element in the product mix. Projections included after-tax earnings of over $10 a share within five years, and a cash flow running double that amount. The analyst was obviously impressed, not only with the information and projections themselves but also with management's candor. Establishment of a congenial after-working-hours rapport was also helpful.

The analyst's report to portfolio managers must have been a favorable one. The action of the stock over the next few days indicated that a large buyer had entered the picture. ABP had stabilized in the 55–60 area, with daily trading now running around 20,000 shares. Some of the offerings close to 60 apparently represented selling by die-hard holders who had taken positions on the Magic run-up over a year back (a misadventure that fortunately had been largely forgotten by now) and were getting out even.

I deduced the presence of a large buyer by a specific behavior pattern. Whenever a large offering appeared, there was always a taker. Thus, for example, during one session ABP was trading in 100- or 300-share lots around 58, followed by an 1,800-share sale at 58¼, then a few 100-share ticks at 58 or 57¾, then later in the day a 2,600-share tick at 58⅛, followed shortly by a 5,000-share block at 58⅝. Each time there was a sizable offering, a buyer was there to take it. At the same time, it was apparent that there was no major competition for blocks of stock. The appearance on the ticker tape of large blocks on upticks would set off a run on the stock, if sizable buyers were competing with one another. The situation now was one of scattered small sellers and traders, and one dominant large buyer.

The entry into the market of the Broad Wall Fund as a buyer of ABP shares could present me with the opportunity I needed to bring my campaign to a successful conclusion. The Fund was a substantial one, with total assets in the $200-million-plus range, and would not be interested in taking an individual stock position totaling less than $5 or $10 million in market value. If I was right that they were the buyers, I could safely count on their wanting at least 100,000 shares. And this would in all probability turn into "locked-up" stock that would not readily reappear for sale just weeks or months later, quick to grab a 10- or 20-point profit.

Moreover, if I could stampede the Fund into urgently bidding up to complete its position in the stock, it could spark a run that would carry ABP to an all-time high, eliminating all problems of stale supply. Further, if the action of the stock were spunky enough, there would not be too much in the way of offerings from profit-takers who had bought the stock at lower prices until it reached much higher levels.

Thus far, the Fund had played it cool. The stock was well bought. The traders for the Fund would take offerings but never chase the stock above the 59 level. There was no necessity to do so, since there was no large competitor seeking shares. My strategy now was to provide that competition, forcing the Fund to stampede to fill its position. But first, I wanted assurance that the Fund had already bought sufficient shares that it would be willing to bid up to get the balance of its targeted position. If the Fund had bought only 25,000 shares or so, and the stock "got away" (moved too high), the

Fund might just decide to change its original investment strategy and instead sell the 25,000 shares on the advance and take a quick profit, rather than chasing the stock up to fill out its position.

So I waited. About two weeks later, my calculations were that the Fund had now accumulated perhaps 60,000 shares and was still buying. It was now close to the middle of the month, right before the short interest figures were to be reported. Each month, five business days after the fifteenth, the New York Stock Exchange releases figures that show the total short interest—the number of shares that have been sold short and not covered by the reporting date (which is actually five business days before the fifteenth). Some traders monitor these figures carefully and will buy a stock that is in new high ground if the short interest has been increasing. Their thinking is that all the shorts have losses and consequently are susceptible to being stampeded into covering their positions by a combination of mounting paper losses and the realization that so many other shorts are in the same boat. Each short seller represents an ultimate purchaser—not one who buys with the objective of reselling later at a higher price— and if shorts are competing to cover, it can become an explosive situation.

In other ways also, the timing was opportune. A board of directors' meeting of ABP was scheduled for the fifteenth. There would doubtless be some good news coming from the meeting, as well as stimuli for the rumor mills seeking an explanation for the stock's strong action.

This excellent market environment would also provide me with an opportunity to close out my option arrangement with Argentte. His call on 25,000 shares at 30 was now six months old. If the stock was called from me at 30 and sold by him on the open market at 60, this would represent a $750,000 profit for him. I told Argentte that I would like him to close out his option position with me. He knew that there was a good chance the stock would go higher, and he knew I felt the same. But I had done him a very generous turn, retrospectively, in bringing him into the situation, and he was not ungrateful. I figured I would kill more than one bird with this stone, and arranged with him that he would offer the 25,000 shares at 60 *short*. I indicated I was confident his stock would be taken on the open market before the week was out. I wanted the 25,000-share short sale to occur in time to show up in the short figures that would be released five business days after the fifteenth.

It was now only two days before the cut-off date for the short figures. The Fund was finding it more difficult to locate substantial offerings in the high 50s and was now nibbling at offerings in the 59–60 area. The pace of buying was still leisurely. There was as yet no large competitor for the shares, but my moment had arrived.

The next morning, about an hour after the market had opened, I placed an order to buy 3,000 shares up to 59¾. The stock moved easily to 59¾ on 2,200 shares, and it was then my bid for 800 additional shares at 59¾ while 31,200 were offered at 60! The bulk of this 31,200-share offering was, of course, the 25,000 shares placed for sale by Argentte, the rest largely represented the round-number psychology again at work, this time among sellers.

A few hundred shares then ticked off at 59⅞ and I waited, a bit excitedly, for a move by the Fund. A rush of scattered traders to take the 60 stock, launching ABP on the way to another jump, was possible, but the large size of the offering made it unlikely. Once a large buyer began nibbling away at the 31,200 shares at 60, traders could jump on the bandwagon, but the offering was probably too big to lure them at the moment. I had no choice, and chanced that the Fund would bite, and bite quickly.

While waiting for what I imagined would be a hurried

call by the Fund's broker on the floor to the Fund's traders to see if they would take the offering at 60, I sold a few hundred shares at the market and withdrew my bid at 59¾. There had been time enough for the Fund's broker to see the 31,200-share offering, and I wanted a downtick or two as a means of staving off a possible assault by floor traders on the 60 stock.

Moments later, a few hundred shares ticked off at 59¾, some small strings at 59⅞ and then 32,400 at 60. I was almost home! Moments later, however, I was to discover that I had outsmarted myself.

18 Out of Control

The Fund had evidently bought the 60 offering and then had sold a few hundred shares immediately afterward. The strategy was to give the casual tape watcher the idea that there was more stock to be sold at 60 and that the buyer had had his fill. My calculation, however, was that by now the Fund had acquired close to 80,000 shares. Either it had filled its position or it was close to doing so. In either case, it was not going to be a seller if the stock ran away. Perhaps it would be a buyer of a few thousand additional shares on the run.

The stock was now ripe for a run-up. It was just after noon and the boardrooms were jammed. ABP had become a well-known and popular star of the Trans-Lux. I immediately placed an order to buy 2,000 shares up to a price of 62. The next ticks were 500 at 60, 500 at 60½, and 1,000 at 61—all my purchases.

Like a revelation, the earlier block of 32,400 shares at 60 was recalled by the full-time boardroom watchers and mentioned by brokers to their customers. The stock was obviously being heavily bought and it was screaming for all to hear: "Buy me, I'm going up." Indeed, this was point-of-purchase advertising at its most irresistible. The impulse buyer was trapped. After all, why do most traders buy a stock? They

133

buy it because it is going up and therefore, by the ineluctable logic of greed, it will continue to go up.

The stock began to trade heavily in 500- and 1,000-share lots around 63 but it had stopped advancing. Suddenly, it became apparent that new sizable sellers or a single large seller had entered the picture and, judging from the action, was mostly short selling. But this wasn't the casual amateur shorting off 100 shares at a time. A test of the market showed shorts were being offered in 1,000-share lots. For the first time since my whole campaign began, I felt mystified and out of control. Frankly, I was also afraid.

A quick call to my associate on the Stock Exchange floor revealed that, at least temporarily, I had outsmarted myself. The floor traders had found out that Argentte had shorted 25,000 shares at 60 as they were hanging around the post where ABP was being traded. They inferred that a shrewd trader like Argentte must have knowledge of some specific negative factor if he was willing to take such a large short position in the stock. Alerted and suspicious, when they saw my attempt to run the stock through 60 by my urgent buy orders, they sensed something was fishy and began to short ABP in 1,000-share lots.

When it began to be obvious to the boardroom traders and daylighters that there were heavy offerings of stock around 63, they began to unload the same shares they had bought only minutes before. ABP backed down to 60, where a few of the floor traders decided to grab a quick profit and cover their short sales made only minutes before at 63. At the close, ABP stood at 61.

For the casual reader of the financial columns the next day, the action of the stock didn't look bad—turnover had soared to 110,000 shares and the stock had made a new high. But to the more sophisticated trader, it was obvious that there was a lot—*too* much—stock for sale. I had been a bit too shrewd. This could prove to be a multimillion-dollar booboo.

I needed some good news, some very good news, to get the stock moving again and discourage the professional shorts. I talked with Confrer that evening. The next morning was to be the directors' meeting. The best news that could be forthcoming would be a stock split accompanied by a higher cash dividend. A startling new breakthrough in forest genetics or a sale of timberlands would have been ideal but could hardly be arranged overnight.

Confrer felt the best strategy was to have Founder III make the proposal of a stock split to the directors, but he was not on particularly amiable terms with Founder, who had objected to the way Confrer had taken the Magic fiasco and the public relations campaign in hand, usurping Founder III's authority. But Founder III's vanity was our trump card. We figured he could be convinced the success of the company and stardom for the stock were all *his* doing and that a proper reward would be a stock split.

Confrer made the call. First, jocular congratulations on the stock's selling at virtually its highest price in history. What else can the shareholders possibly want, except a split? mused Confrer. To my surprise and infinite relief, Founder III jumped to the bait. That was just what he was thinking— "You'll back the idea at the directors' meeting in the morning, eh, Confrer?" It was all too easy. Founder III surely had something up his sleeve. Bonanza of bonanzas, so he did!

Founder III was all smiles at the nine-thirty board meeting the next morning. The monthly operations review was quickly dispensed with. Founder III congratulated the directors on their superb stewardship of the company (they had rubber-stamped every one of his proposals for years) and then proposed a two-for-one split and an increase in the cash dividend. The rate on the new stock would be $0.20 quarterly, or the equivalent of a boost from $0.35 to $0.40 on the old shares. The proposal was quickly and unanimously approved and the secretary of the corporation was dispatched immediately to inform the Stock Exchange to hold up trading while the news was released and disseminated.

ABP had opened fractionally above 60 and then encountered heavy short selling in the initial few minutes of the session, to sink back to 59 when trading was temporarily suspended for the split announcement. The news immediately sparked public interest, and the stock ran easily back to 63 before the floor traders once again began to pummel it with short offerings. It managed to hold on to some of its gain, closing at 61½ on turnover of 52,000 shares for the day.

The directors' meeting continued after the split proposal and approval, and Founder III's strategy became more apparent. "Gentlemen, our stock had now risen to a level that is closer to reflecting the true value of our company. We can now use it as payment to acquire concerns that will round out our product line and provide us with entry into more dynamic, faster-growing segments of the economy." He continued by then revealing that he had come across Copytronics, a small producer of coated paper used in copying machines that had developed a new type of electrostatic copier. The machine could be mass-produced at a cost well below comparable Xerox models.

Copytronics, however, was short of capital and did not have the financial or managerial resources necessary to build up the vast sales, distribution, and service network required for success in the industry. Founder III had talked with directors of Copytronics and they were amenable to a merger for stock, believing that an alliance with the "formidable management skills and substantial capital resources of ABP" would be mutually beneficial.

One might imagine that the collective memory of the board of directors would immediately flash back to the Magic acquisition. Would this be another case of ABP overpaying to get a tiny position in an industry it knew nothing about and where it had absolutely no competitive advantage? No,

Founder III, having taken credit for the stock's rise to its present eminence, had visions of growth and glamour dancing before their eyes. Copytronics would be another Xerox (just as Magic Transistor should have become another Texas Instruments after *its* acquisition) and capital gains would cover the earth!

The balance sheets of Copytronics and the proposed terms of the deal were presented to the board. For Copytronics's sales of about $6 million in copying paper and profits of some $300,000, ABP was to issue 200,000 shares with a market value then of about $12 million.

This bit of folly was to be a godsend for me. Everything was now in harmony again. The stock was near an all-time high, the short interest had expanded substantially, including a lot of participation from professionals, and the best seemed yet to come. I decided to help things along by placing an order for 200 call options (for 20,000 shares) with a major put-and-call option broker. I was bidding only $500 per call, knowing that I would not be able to get any calls at that low price. But one of the best ways to start rumors of "smart buying" is for the word to get out that there is substantial demand for calls on a stock.

By now, however, ABP had gotten out of my control, and my help was no longer needed. The stock opened with a bang the next session, which was the same day on which the short interest would be reported after the close. The initial trade was a large one: 35,000 shares at 64, where numerous small speculative buyers were matched with numerous traders taking profits, but this time there would be no professional shorts to contain the rise. They were still suspicious of the stock, but it was acting much better than they thought it should had something been wrong. Perhaps old Argentte had been taken in, or had pulled one off against the shorts. The professionals began to feel they had been had, but they weren't going to cover in the midst of a public stampede for the stock.

Part of the strength in the stock's performance was attributable to the spreading of a story about a "huge merger in the copying field." Some versions had it that Xerox would take over ABP on a handsome share-exchange deal. This was being rationalized as being a step toward backward integration (to the source of paper) by Xerox.

19 Distribution

I guess we all yearn for clear cause-and-effect relationships to explain otherwise mysterious happenings. It is never enough to say that a mob of irrational people want a stock for a variety of irrational, often unrationalized motives, and so a stock advances. That is no answer—although often, the only explanation may be that a stock goes up because it is going up because it is going up. But, that is not a satisfactory reason for most people. There must be a story, again often accompanied by an omniscient "they," who have superior wisdom and are therefore more competent appraisers of the stock. The pathetic identity crisis that is plaguing professionals as well as amateurs on Wall Street stems from a quixotic attempt to impose a rational discipline upon an irrational institution.

And thus it was with ABP. Instead of being just another name lost in anonymity among a thousand others that crowded the pages of stock tabulations in the *Wall Street Journal*, ABP was now a cynosure of traders, investors, and speculators. Frequently on the most active list, alluringly volatile, and commanding the allegiance of universally delighted shareowners, here was a new luminary on Wall Street. In addition to the Xerox merger rumor, there were stories about a huge oil find in the Mississippi property and stor-

139

ies of secret sales of tens of thousands of acres of timberland, for thousands of dollars per acre. After all, ABP owned 100,000-plus acres of timberland. At thousands per, the timberlands alone could be worth half a billion dollars.

There were also stories of smart Swiss buying. As a matter of fact, a broker friend of mine did execute a buy order for a Geneva client who bought 2,000 shares at 64—to cover a short sale made two months before at substantially lower prices.

In a frantic search for the why behind the sudden stardom for ABP shares, the chemical research subsidiary now became a hot topic of conversation. According to some self-confessed authorities, the subsidiary had successfully developed a proprietary method to double the rate of growth for trees. This immediately made ABP's timberlands even more valuable, and gave ABP a competitive edge that would ultimately drive everyone else out of the wood products industry. And the development had dramatic possibilities in agriculture and cattle raising.

But probably the heaviest buying of the stock came from friends of Founder III, whose enthusiasm about the Copytronics merger was contagious. Founder III was niggardly —and rightly so—with statistics on current earnings. But he was generous indeed with projections that called for a 20% share of a $10-billion-dollar market in a matter of years. And most importantly, Founder III was now a proven winner. His stock had doubled in only months, was at an all-time high, and was one of the most talked-about and eagerly sought "investments" on the big board.

An acquaintance of mine, whom I had advised to buy ABP stock some months before, called me during this period to return the favor. He hadn't followed my advice then, when the stock was half its present price. He had decided to "watch the stock for a while," and he was now buying ABP and was going to let me in on some very confidential information about what was really going on at the company. According to him, ABP had signed three deals to acquire companies in the photocopy and computer fields, acquisitions that would add over $2 to share earnings. Of course, I knew the information was false—even assuming there were three acquisitions, no deal could be entered into without approval of the directors. And they had just received the proposal on Copytronics for their decision the preceding week.

My acquaintance swore me to secrecy, confiding that he had gotten the information from one of the ABP directors, a close personal friend. I doubted if he knew any of the directors. He had probably picked up some version of the story in a boardroom and embellished it (perhaps unconsciously) with each retelling, meanwhile adding to his own consequence by announcing that a director was his personal source. It happens every day.

The multitude of rumors and the performance of the stock were now prominent in the financial sections of the newspapers. The reporter who covers Wall Street is in an impossible position: He can't simply say ABP jumped $3 because buyers felt more urgency than did sellers. His readers demand that he give a reason, and one can always be found for the credulous.

Several reporters called the company and were referred to the public relations director, who, by now, had a very handsome unrealized profit on his options on ABP stock. He told the reporters that there were no plans for an *immediate* sale of additional timberlands but did confirm publicly that the Michigan property had gone for $10,000 an acre and that the company owned well over 100,000 additional acres. True, drilling had begun on the Mississippi properties, but any information on its progress would have to be forthcoming from the lessee oil company that was to do the drilling. True, the chemical subsidiary was making excellent progress, but it was company policy not to announce new products until they were sufficiently beyond the development stage to be of significance to operations. As for the Copytronics acquisition, "ABP is continually on the lookout for advantageous acquisitions that would enhance its growth potential and has a number under consideration at the present time."

These comments, once translated into dream language, would read: ABP advances on substantial gains possible from timberlands sales. Major oil company secretive on Mississippi exploration to deter competitors. Street awaits marketing plans for new products of chemical subsidiary. ABP considering important acquisitions in growth areas.

And now came the short interest figures. Bolstered by Argentte's 25,000 shares, the total short interest had leaped to almost 80,000 shares. With ABP now in all-time high ground of 70, every shareholder was happy and not anxious to sell while the stock was still going up. So the shorts were in trouble—each had a sizable loss and was vulnerable to being stampeded into covering his position.

On the news of the short interest, ABP ran to 76. Trading soared to over 150,000 shares, of which I sold about a third. In the following few sessions, I unloaded most of the balance of my position in the mid-70s and was now down to about 30,000 shares. This was going to be supplied to buyers on the final bit of "good news" the following week, when the board of directors, in all probability, would approve the acquisition of Copytronics.

The directors' meeting was scheduled for four-thirty on the next Tuesday. The stock had been trading heavily in the mid-70s. It ran to a new high on Tuesday, reaching 78, but had closed at the low of the day, 74, on a whopping turnover of 175,000 shares. It was obvious to me that the stock was close to a point of exhausting the demand for it. Virtually everyone who wanted to buy it had already done so, except for perhaps 60,000 shorts, who still held to their uncomfortable positions. I booked passage on the U.S.S. *Constitution* for a vacation trip to Europe leaving Wednesday night, for my campaign was to be over that Tuesday afternoon.

The figures on Copytronics that were presented to the directors would have dismayed anyone not intoxicated with the spectacular performance of ABP stock. But the directors, like Founder III himself, had somehow come to believe in Wall Street's exalted valuation of their entrepreneurial talents. The market says ABP is a great company, and the market knows best. At present market valuation, ABP was going to give some $15 million in stock for $6 million in sales, $300,000 in profits, and a machine that was still in the development stage! Copytronics had no distribution system and no sales force for the new machine—building these up would entail huge expenses and large losses for some time. Sales and service were the key to success in this industry. It was indisputable that Copytronics could offer neither, and problematical whether it had a product.

But Founder III gave an alluring presentation. This was the growth area of the future. Founder III stressed the stock market's positive reaction to rumors of the acquisition— something the directors were well aware of. That inviolate receptacle of wisdom, The Marketplace, had spoken: The acquisition was right. Flush with the inflated value of their stock options, well aware of what superstar Xerox had done on the stock market, the directors approved. The price was high on the now, but they felt they were guilty of almost stealing Copytronics in view of its hereafter.

The release of the announcement on the acquisition was timed to hit the late news wires. The financial pages of the newspapers the following morning were full of the story. The influx of buy orders in ABP was so great on Wednesday that the opening in the stock was delayed until around noon. Before the opening, I had put in my order to sell my remaining 30,000 shares at the market. My offering would limit the size of the gap in price above the previous night's closing of 74 and perhaps restrain any explosive force in the stock, but I was now anticipating the end of my campaign. I was desirous that it be over. I had made a large investment of capital, effort, emotion, and, yes, anxiety in the situation. As the campaign approached completion, I was feeling drained by the excitement. Moreover, everything was now going too well and my trader's instinct told me to be quick and take advantage of these ideal circumstances.

The stock did open with a bang: 65,000 shares at 77. Few shorts would sell ABP now, as none was left with that much courage. I felt that in all probability this would be within a point or so of the top price for ABP. All the good news was out. Everyone who urgently wanted to own the stock now owned it, and subsequent buyers would wait for lower prices. Logically, the stock had no where to go but down.

One thing I have learned in this business, though, is that while stocks may ultimately sell in a reasonable relationship to objective standards of value, there is no way of quantifying the degree of overvaluation or undervaluation that can result when speculative fever or fearful pessimism engulfs an issue. Overcrowded situations—going either up or down— have a way of overreaching themselves. There were still quite a few shorts in ABP, maybe more came in that day at the opening.

But everyone who owned the stock was happy—ABP was at an all-time high. Maybe the magic of Copytronics would hold the stock at this level, or push it higher for a period of weeks, months, or even years before the owners of the stock realized it was a losing proposition. The operating outlook for the company was now unpredictable. Founder would obviously savor *his* apparent stock market coup achieved by the merger, and frenzied speculators now dominated the action of the stock. ABP's stock had already lost a reasonable relationship to traditional standards of value, so why couldn't it sell at 107 instead of 77?

I would eventually return from my trip and go back to the arena. If I wanted to short ABP then, I could do so, and it could be a better short lower and on the way down than at 77 and on the way up.

Knowing that my stock was sold at the opening, I gave my office instructions to place the total proceeds of all sales for myself and customers into short-term Treasury bills. I was in a hurry to pack and board the *Constitution*.

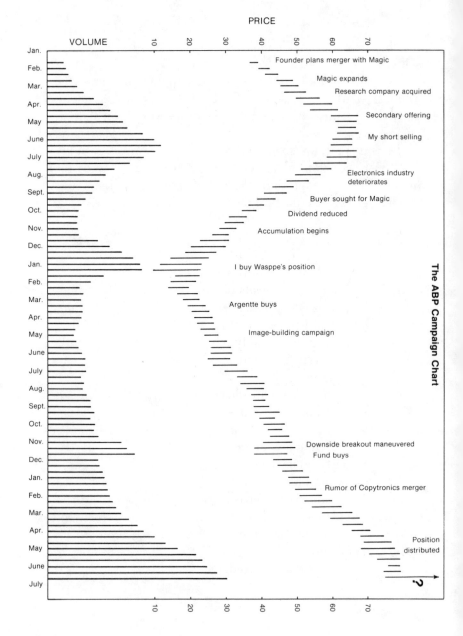

PRICE

VOLUME

The ABP Campaign Chart

Founder plans merger with Magic

Magic expands

Research company acquired

Secondary offering

My short selling

Electronics industry deteriorates

Buyer sought for Magic

Dividend reduced

Accumulation begins

I buy Wasppe's position

Argentte buys

Image-building campaign

Downside breakout maneuvered

Fund buys

Rumor of Copytronics merger

Position distributed

Epilogue

By midafternoon I had finished my packing, boarded the *Constitution*, and was comfortably ensconced in my cabin. I had no financial commitments pending and expected no communication from my office. My clients had been informed that the campaign had been successfully completed and that their funds were resting comfortably but not idly in Treasury bills, waiting for my return to the investment arena at some indefinite future date.

I was about to take a nap when the steward knocked at my cabin door and brought me a telegram. I was more puzzled than alarmed and opened it quickly. The message was from my office: "Oil company announces major find on ABP Mississippi property. Bon voyage."

Now, everyone was happy. ABP had provided me and my clients with a sumptuous repast, one a bit too heavily spiced for some appetites. I had no regrets at having perhaps left dessert on the table for those who had taken me out of my investment position.

It was a delightful trip indeed.